Treading Water

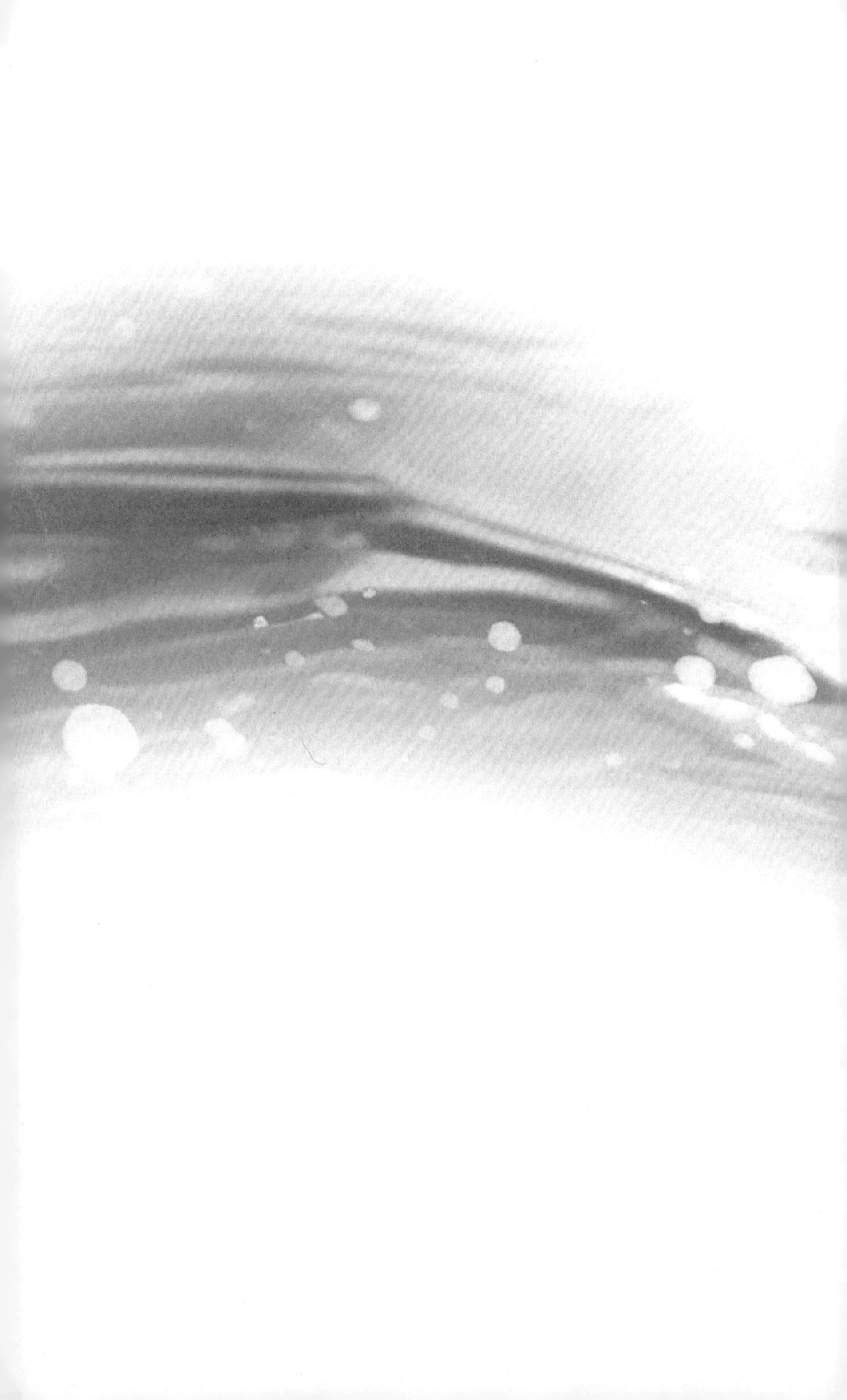

For Helen, a dear friend

Treading Water

Blessings of endurance always!

Love
Patrice
3-6-24

PATRICE MOYES COUCH

SUNSHINE FAMILY PUBLISHING

Treading Water

For information contact:
grandmatrice@gmail.com

Published by:
Sunshine Family Publishing

Copy Editor: Toni Asay • Content Editor: Kim Autrey
Cover design by elQue.design • 99designs
Interior book design by Francine Platt, Eden Graphics, Inc.

Paperback ISBN 978-1-958626-62-7
Ebook ISBN 978-1-958626-83-2

Library of Congress Number: Pending

First Edition

DEDICATION

To MY CHILDREN, Michelle and Chad, who grew up as beautiful adults and parents. They both inspire me every day.

ALSO, TO MY TWO BONUS DAUGHTERS, Patricia and Amanda, who share the love of their dad with me.

To MY HUSBAND, Roger, who after forty-four years apart decided that it might be fun to give us another chance.

LAST, TO A DEAR FRIEND, Rita Davenport, who unbeknownst to her, saved my life many years ago by letting me know through her books and audiotapes I could be a "Who's Who!" instead of a "What's That?" I listened to her recordings so often my daughter started calling her Aunt Rita, and I even think I started talking with a little southern drawl.

FOREWORD

by Rita Davenport

I MET PATRICE many years ago as a consultant for Arbonne Skin Care. I was grateful when she shared with me how I had been such a strong example to her in the mid-80s as she was struggling with her life. She said she listened to my audio recordings and read my books so many times she even started talking with a little southern drawl. One day her daughter came home from school, and Patrice was listening to one of my recordings. Her daughter's friend said, "WHO is that your mom is listening to?" Michelle said, "Oh, that is just Aunt Rita!"

I have on several occasions through the past several years had the opportunity to become friends with Patrice and her brother, Jerry. I have been impressed at her strength to overcome her struggles and always looking for ways to help others and not judge others. Her philanthropy work is remarkable. She does so much to help so many.

She has written this book to help her family and others know the challenges she faced and why and how she made certain choices in her life and the reasons she did so. She is remarkable and strong. Her example is inspiring.

I hope you as a reader will be able to feel her love and appreciation for her life and the challenges she has faced and the lives she has touched. Her book will make a difference for so many to give others inspiration.

PROLOGUE

I AM NO ONE REALLY IMPORTANT. I am not writing this book to be a *New York Times* Bestseller. I am a wife, a mother, a grandma, a great-grandma, a sister, a niece, an aunt, a cousin, and a friend. It is my wish for my family, friends, and anyone else reading this to know the real me—the me that went from a young, struggling twenty-six-year-old single mother with absolutely no self-worth, contemplating taking my life, to the me that has the self-confidence to share my journey by writing and being able to speak to thousands of people.

In doing research for this book, I have searched the "archives of time," going through old files. I have kept every talk and presentation I have ever given. There are two common words that seem to resonate through them all: gratitude and resilience.

Knowing there is a little girl still inside of me, it has been very emotional to see the growth and not really know when or where the genuine changes came.

This book is not a memoir about my life. It is a compilation of different times in my life that helped shape me into the woman I am today and the lessons I learned along the way. The stories aren't necessarily in any order of importance. Each story I share has impacted my life immensely in one way or another.

I have learned forgiveness, both of myself and others, tolerance, integrity, and humility. I have learned how to be more generous, how to grieve, how to both give and receive service, how to love others, and also how to learn to love myself along the journey.

Every time I would share with others the different stories of my life, some would gasp in awe, some would laugh so hard they would cry, and others would agree with my mother. She always said I had nine lives.

In June 2022, I was able to attend a writer's retreat at the Timepiece Ranch in Southern Utah. Author Richard Paul Evans was the host.

In my individual time with Richard, he asked me what my dream for my book was. I said, "Something to make my family proud of my life and decisions I have made throughout it." He said, "What is one word?" I said, "Oh, I don't know, maybe—survival?" He suggested, "How about resilience?"

I shared my Treasure Island story with him, and he said, "That is where you should start, with a possible title, *Treading Water*." He asked me to have a rough draft by January 2023.

Resilience! The capacity to withstand or quickly recover from difficult conditions, or, being able to recoil or spring back into shape after bending, stretching, or being compressed.[1] Yes, that's me!

In this book, *Treading Water*, I am sharing the different and sometimes difficult times in my life where I have been resilient both learning to love and to be loved.

My dear friend, Jennifer Riggs, wrote, "We all have a story we tell ourselves about who we are and what our life is like. The really amazing thing is that we have the power to choose the story we tell and that will change our reality."

Everyone has a story. So mine begins…

CHAPTER 1

The most difficult decisions are often not the ones in which we cannot determine the correct course, rather the ones to which we are certain of the path, but fear the journey.

– Richard Paul Evans, *The Locket*

THE WATER WAS WARM and dark. As I worked my way out of the partially submerged car through the driver's side window, all I could taste was salty water, and all I could think was, "Where am I?" The date was October 7, 1976, midnight, Treasure Island, Florida, and the movie *JAWS* had just been released.

While I was treading water trying to figure out what had just happened, the car's taillights went out, and the car was completely submerged.

Earlier that day…

The morning started as a very stressful day for me. My marriage was in shambles, crumbling right before my eyes. I was struggling for my very existence. My husband, Mark, and I were living in Phoenix, Arizona. I was a stay-at-home mom with a five-year-old daughter and a two-year-old son.

We had been struggling for several months because of my husband's extra-marital relationships. Divorce wasn't in my vocabulary because I did not want to be a single mother.

Religion had never been an important factor in our marriage. I was an inactive member of the Church of Jesus Christ of Latter-day Saints, and he was a Southern Baptist.

His family was living in Tampa, Florida, and had become involved with a church based in Pasadena, California, The Worldwide Church of God. This religion followed the Holy Days from the Old Testament.

We had traveled this particular week to St. Petersburg, Florida, to be with his family for The Feast of Tabernacles, a weeklong conference of sermons, sermonettes, music, and prayer.

I hated being there because I didn't believe in WHY we were there—to celebrate the Holy Days with his parents, who never thought I was good enough for their son.

However, on this day, a minister gave a sermonette, a short version of a lengthy sermon. He started it out with a story of three young adult girls who had decided to climb a dangerous mountain. As they began their ascent, a storm started to roll in. They were determined to continue to the top, but after several hours decided they needed to turn back. Shortly after they started back down, one of the girls started to struggle and said she couldn't go any longer. Her friends pleaded with her to continue back with them, but she eventually gave up. As the other two friends continued their descent, she remained behind. They knew as they told her goodbye they may never see her again, but they also knew they had to continue back down. The two girls made it back safely because of their intense desire and quest to endure to the end and not give up. Sadly, their friend perished in the storm.

As the minister walked from the podium, I was so touched. I could not tell you another sermon or sermonette I heard during that week, but his words hit my heart. ENDURE TO THE END!

That night, Mark and I got away for a while and went to a movie. I had asked some friends to stay with our children for the evening at our hotel.

Surprisingly, in spite of the conflicts in our marriage, we had a peaceful, enjoyable evening and were looking for a place to eat on our way back to Treasure Island.

On the toll road between St. Petersburg and Treasure Island, the road separated and came back together several times. As we passed through the final toll booth in our rented red 1977 Cutlass Oldsmobile, Mark threw the coins in the basket and undid his seat belt. I thought that was strange. He also left his window down.

As we came over the small rise at the beginning of a bridge, suddenly, he accelerated, started screaming, and drove us into the Boca Ciega Bay. I remember thinking, "This is a dream! This can't be happening!" We hit the water about seventy-five feet from the shore. Our windshield broke on impact, and the car started to sink. With his window down and his seat belt unfastened, Mark immediately got out of the car and started swimming to the shore, not knowing if I was out or not. I was able to unbuckle my seatbelt and get out of the car through his window, having no idea what body of water I was in or where I was.

As I was treading water, the thought came to me, "Just give up. You can just float away, and you will be free from all of your troubles." I then thought of my two children, back in the hotel with a babysitter they didn't even know, and suddenly, the minister's sermonette about enduring to the end came to my mind. I realized I needed to fight to stay alive. And I had to fight hard! Just then the taillights went out, and the car completely submerged.

I could hear sirens and looked over at the shore. There were lights lining the bridge. Several fire trucks and a few spectators had gathered on the shore. I could see a nurse in a white uniform standing at the edge of the water. She yelled out to me, asking if I was okay. I yelled back I was but to keep an eye on me because I couldn't swim very well. I had a three-piece wool pantsuit on that was weighing me down. I could swim in a clear, beautiful pool, but, again, I had no idea what body of water I was even in.

I finally got to the shore, and the firemen pulled me up the six-foot seawall. They wrapped me in blankets and made sure I was all right.

They asked me what happened, and I told them my husband just started screaming and drove us into the water. I later found out he had told them another car had forced him off the road, but there were some young boys who had been on the bridge on their bikes and had witnessed us going into the water. They said there was not another car on the road, and he had just started screaming and drove into the water.

I remember looking around and asking where the nurse was who had yelled out to me. Perhaps, maybe, she had seen something. No one else had seen her, and they dismissed it, saying she must have just been a motorist passing by and stopped to see if she could help.

We were taken by ambulance to the local hospital. Mark had hurt his knee in the accident, but I didn't have any injuries. I went into the tiny emergency room bathroom to take off my heavy, wet clothes. I noticed as I took off my bra something I thought was seaweed was covering my left breast. As I looked down, I realized it was chipped glass. I assumed it had gone down my neck on impact. Chipped, broken glass was embedded in my entire breast. I hollered for the emergency room nurse, and when she came in, she couldn't believe what she saw. She gave me a towel and carefully helped me remove and gently brush all the glass onto the floor. Not one piece of glass had cut me, and there was not a drop of blood.

We called our friends and asked them to pick us up from the hospital and take us back to our hotel.

Looking back on this now, thinking about the state of our marriage, the elements that led up to the accident, Mark not having his seat belt on, rolling his window down, and the fact he never once looked back to see if I was even out of the car or okay, was just one more thing I had to struggle with over the years. Was he trying to harm me?

Our marriage didn't survive much longer.

A few years later, I was talking to a friend about my experience and the accident, and she took ahold of my hand and said, "Pat, do you think the nurse on the shore that night in Florida had been your guardian angel?" I laughed and said, "Oh, there is no such thing as guardian angels!"

CHAPTER 2

When your butt's a 'draggin', keep your head up high!

– Grandma Gladys, my mother's mother

I graduated from Weber High School in 1968. I had received a Nursing Scholarship from the local community college in Salt Lake but decided instead to go to Weber State College in Ogden. As the winter quarter ended, my brother, Jerry, called me one morning and asked me what I was going to do for spring break. I told him I didn't have any plans, and he asked if I wanted to come to Phoenix and work with him for a few weeks. He had just fired his secretary and needed some help. So, I told him yes, I would come. "But only for two weeks," I said. Well, ten years, a marriage, a divorce, and two kids later, I moved back to Plain City.

I was the third employee of what is now Swift Transportation. This was a family owned business that was started by my brother Jerry. When I began working in 1969, we had four trucks. At that time, it was called Common Market Distributing Corporation. There were lots of changes and growth that took place over the next several years.

My job was to keep track of the trucks in a "truck record" book—where they were going, what they were hauling, who they were hauling for, and what their delivery places and times were. I also did simple bookkeeping and payroll. There were a few times I would babysit if the drivers needed help with their children.

Those days were very simple and lean. I remember many days I would take one driver with me to the bank to make a business deposit so that he could cash his paycheck in the line behind me. In those early days, we were all like family with the drivers. My mother was always in charge of the monthly reports, and even years after she quit working, she would always panic on the twenty-fifth of every month and wonder if whoever was in charge of reports got them mailed on time. Even now, I will once in a while, on the twenty-fifth of a month, smile and think of my mom.

Shortly after I moved to Phoenix, I quickly decided I wasn't going back to Plain City, even though I would get so homesick. I had the *Ogden Standard Examiner* newspaper mailed to me, and it would arrive two days late. The men at the post office got to know me and knew how excited I was every day to get the paper, even though it was two days late. Many days when I would go pick up the mail, I would catch one of them sitting with his legs up on his desk reading MY paper. They would laugh and laugh and sometimes would actually be laughing at some of the stories.

One day at work, I had a major conflict with a coworker and was crying. As I walked past my dad in the hallway, he could see I was visibly upset, but he didn't say a word.

Traveling home after work, I stopped at my parents' home. My mother had been watching my children that day because my usual sitter was ill. When I got there, I shared with Mother what had happened earlier in the day. We visited for a while, and she felt bad for my hard day. I took the kids and went home.

When my dad got home that evening, my mother told him about our conversation and what had happened at work. He called me later that night and told me to stop by in the morning, he wanted to talk to me. I dropped off the kids the following morning at our normal sitter and went to see my dad. We sat down at their dining room table. He asked me how much money I made. I told him I made $350.00 a month. He said, "All right, you're done! Your brothers' wives don't have to work." He slammed his palm on the table and said, "and by God, neither do you! Your job is to raise your kids. I'm going to keep you on the payroll, so you have an income and insurance, but you're done."

Several weeks later, I sold my home, took my two kids, Michelle and Chad, and left Phoenix. I knew as a single mom I could never compete with my brothers and their families. I moved back to my hometown, Plain City, Utah, and I continued to get my $350.00 a month for several more years—even after my dad died.

I often wonder where I would have been in life had I decided to stay in Phoenix and work for the family business, but I have truly never regretted leaving.

CHAPTER 3

A mother's love for her child is like nothing else in the world. It knows no law, no pity, it dares all things and crushes down remorselessly all that stands in its path.

– Agatha Christie, *The Hound of Death: And Other Stories*

I recently heard of a dear friend who suffered from a condition known as transient global amnesia. It is a neurological disorder whose key defining characteristic is a temporary but almost total disruption of short-term memory.

There are several known causes for this disorder, but one is stressful conditions. Hearing of my dear friend's condition took me back to 1984, when I experienced something like this. My condition was diagnosed as a venous angioma, most likely caused when one of the veins in my head had burst. Could have been stress related, they said.

I was struggling with my second marriage, building a new home, a daughter who thought life would be better living in California with her dad, my mom's recent major surgery, and my dad, who was suffering from prostate cancer.

I was working full time and trying to be a good wife and mother. One night, I remember coming down the hallway in our home. My kids were fighting, and my husband was upset with them. Everything just seemed so wrong. As I turned the corner to go up the stairs, I just collapsed. Later, I remember telling them, "None of you are worth my life!" I felt like they were destroying me emotionally and physically.

The next day, I was at work, and just before lunch, I experienced something that felt like a bomb going off in my head and then a burst of what seemed like sparklers in my head. It left almost as fast as it came on. The lady I was working with told me I just grabbed my head and screamed.

We went to lunch, but I had no appetite. By the time I got back to work, I was numb on the right side of my face and my upper right thigh, and I had a severe headache. I went immediately to the hospital and had a CAT scan. They wanted me back the following morning for another CAT scan with dye, and the next day for something new called an MRI. It was the MRI that finally diagnosed my issue as a venous angioma. Considering all the stress I had, I agreed with the diagnosis—it certainly may have been stress related.

The prescribed medication had terrible effects on me. It made me feel like I was in a dark place. Yet, I was told I would most likely be on it for the rest of my life. Shortly after that, one of my doctors left the state, and my other doctor took his own life. These events left me with a year-long prescription of a drug I hated and an unknown future. After the year was up, my pharmacist told me he no longer could fill the prescription, and I would need a new one. I decided I had to find a new neurologist. When I finally got in for an appointment, I explained I had no idea where my records were and told him everything I could remember about my previous treatment.

He told me I never should have been put on that medication, and he took me off it—cold turkey. That was indeed a gigantic leap of faith for me, because I had been told by three different doctors, I would need to be on it for the rest of my life. I never had any complications from being taken off the drug.

During this time, I had worked as a skin care consultant for Arbonne Skin Care, and at one of the national conventions, I realized the newest district and area managers got to go on stage and be recognized with the owner, Petter Morck. I decided at the next convention, I was going to be that newest district manager. And guess what? I was! But what I traded that recognition and hard work for was my marriage. I wanted love, respect, and recognition, and he said he just wanted a wife. Life is a choice.

This marriage was failing also, and I was facing divorce # 2.

My husband, Jay, was a good man, and we had some good, fun years together, but eventually, we were divorced, and life went on.

I often tell others that in this marriage we both hit midlife crisis together and didn't have the strength to hang on.

CHAPTER 4

Do the things that interest you and do them with all your heart. Don't be concerned about whether people are watching you or criticizing you. The chances are that they aren't paying any attention to you. It's your attention to yourself that is so stultifying. But you have to disregard yourself as completely as possible. If you fail the first time then you'll just have to try harder the second time. After all, there's no real reason why you should fail. Just stop thinking about yourself.

– Eleanor Roosevelt,
You Learn by Living: Eleven Keys for a More Fulfilling Life

After two failed marriages, I had decided I would never get married again! Several friends were always trying to set me up with dates, and I had a fun singles group I ran around with. Life was good. Then one day, my friend's son said to me he really wanted me to meet his boss. I wasn't interested but asked him what his boss's name was. He said, "Jeff Archibald." I smiled and said, "Jeff Archibald? I went to school with him. He's single again? Sure, I'll go out with him. Give him my number."

We met, dated, had a short courtship. and were married in November 1995.

We truly struggled our first several years. He had been in a bad relationship, which had taken him to some dark places emotionally, mentally, and physically. He also had lost his job right before we were married, and he really struggled to find his niche in life.

As the years went by, our marriage still had struggles and some hiccups along the way, but we had settled into a groove. We were so different in so many ways. Many days I just wanted out of the marriage.

After he got his job at SME Steel working in Human Resources, he got some of his self-esteem back and poured everything he had into his job. He loved his job and was loved and respected by his coworkers. We were finally at a good place in our marriage.

On December 1, 2007, Jeff and I woke up to over a foot of snow. We got up, had breakfast, and went to do some Christmas shopping. We were gone most of the day. When we came home, we were going to unload the car and go buy our first live Christmas tree.

He decided he would hurry and snow blow the walks, so I started unloading the car. Our son-in-law, Billy, and two grandsons, Chancler and Kaden, were there. Billy helped me unload the car, and the boys were sledding in our backyard. We had the perfect sledding hill, and they were having so much fun. I started watching the boys out our back window and laughing at their antics.

Jeff didn't come in for quite a while, so I went out to check on him, thinking he was chatting with a neighbor. He was just coming to the front of the walk and, as he turned around, the snow was hitting the side of the house. Smiling, I motioned to him with my hand turning in circles and pointing to the house for him to turn the blower, so it wasn't hitting the house. He grinned, nodded, reached down, and turned the blower away from the house. I went back into the house. That was my last interaction with him.

Several more minutes passed, and again, I wondered why he hadn't come back into the house. He surely should have been finished by now. I looked out my kitchen window and saw him on the sidewalk—flat on his back, and his face was ashen blue! Billy was making the boys some hot chocolate, so I yelled to him Jeff was hurt. He ran outside as I called 911. Jeff had suffered a major heart attack.

The paramedics transported him to Davis Regional Hospital, and I followed with his son, Shane, in his vehicle.

We were all in shock as we gathered at the hospital. Dear friends and neighbors also came to support us.

I kept wondering where my daughter, Michelle, was, and why she and Billy hadn't come to the hospital yet. What I didn't realize until days later was because Billy was the first on the scene of an unaccompanied death, they made him stay on the scene until the hospital let the police know it had indeed been a heart attack. Billy could then leave my home and come to the hospital. That broke my heart for Billy because I knew of his love and concern for Jeff.

Jeff had always said he wanted to be an organ donor. While we were all gathered outside his room, the hospital coordinator came to me and told me Intermountain Donor Services was on the line and wanted to speak to me. Just then, his son, Shane, who was a deputy sheriff and EMT, came out of the room and said Jeff was indeed gone, and they had done everything they could for him.

They rushed me immediately into a little cubicle with Intermountain Donor Services on the phone. Did I agree to…her voice seemed to be in the far distance. Heart? "No!" Eyes? "No!" She continued listing body parts like it was a grocery list. I remember saying yes to everything else. She then said, "Okay, now what about large tissues?" I did not know what she meant by that. She said, "Major bones, skin…" I told her she had to stop, and I needed to have my family with me for these decisions. We all gathered in another small room to discuss this. Our dear friend, Larene Jaques, who was like another grandma to my grandkids, had recently had a kidney transplant, so we knew the importance of organ donations. We all agreed we could be the family on the other side of the wall waiting for an organ for a loved one, so, collectively, we agreed to allow them to take whatever they could use.

A few nights before he passed away was our twelfth anniversary. We were at the Timbermine Restaurant in Ogden, enjoying a lovely meal. He took hold of my hand and told me he knew he hadn't been the easiest guy to live with but thanked me for "the wild ride!"

The morning of his funeral was very stressful as we were all trying to get ready. We held it at the Layton East Stake Center near our home.

I was at the church waiting for the mortuary hearse to arrive, which was running late. The time was getting close to begin the services, and they still hadn't arrived with his body. We assumed they were lost. Just then, my grandson, who was still at our house, called me and said, kind of stammering, "Ah, oh, Grandpa just went by the house going the wrong direction. I think the driver is lost." We all laughed so hard. Just as I was calling the mortuary, he called again and said, "Oh, there goes Grandpa again. I think they will be there in a minute." It was just like Jeff to be late for his own funeral so that we could all have a last laugh at his antics. It was a beautiful funeral with over one thousand people in attendance.

The hours, days, and weeks that followed were so hard. I had several people who would comment to me they didn't feel like I had grieved enough. This really angered me because I didn't show a lot of emotion, but like I would tell them, they weren't with me in the car when I heard a certain song on the radio or sitting alone at night in the house.

One night, I was alone in the house sitting on my living room sofa crying. It had been a hard day. I was missing my mother and Jeff. I remember just falling over to the side of the couch. Suddenly, I felt arms around me in comfort. It startled me. No one was there.

This taught me to never judge how someone shows grief after losing a loved one and to always show love, understanding, and respect because everyone grieves so differently.

The day after Jeff's funeral, our Stake President, Mark Gilliland, called my son, Chad, and told him because of our Stake Conference that weekend, there was a General Authority visiting and did he think I would be up for a visit from them? The General Authority's name was Ronald Rasband. We actually had to look in the church magazine, *Ensign*, to see who he was.

President Gilliland and Elder Rasband came to my home the following day, and we felt so much comfort from their visit. My kids and grandkids were there, and I received a beautiful blessing from Elder Rasband before he left. A few years later, he was called to be one of the 12 Apostles in our church. I will always have a special place in my heart for him and the time he took to come and comfort our family.

When Jeff died, we were at a wonderful place in our marriage. I can honestly say I had no regrets.

Now, after two divorces and the death of a husband, I thought I was done. Done with dating and marriage. I did, however, start dating some and again doing some traveling.

Then…

CHAPTER 5

Sometimes you have to let go of the picture of what you thought life would be like and learn to find joy in the story you're actually living.

– Rachel Marie Martin, *Facebook*, November 3, 2023

The morning of January 24, 2013, started just like any other morning in Phoenix, Arizona. My mother had passed away in 2002, and I had inherited her home there. I loved spending time there and visiting with old friends, my son, his wife, and my grandkids.

The sun was brilliant, and my birds were out in full abundance. "My birds," as I called them, were doves. My mother always loved them and had several feeders around her yard. When I would come visit, I would set out the terra cotta bowls and fill them with birdseed. They would all line up on the roofline of the neighbor's house and wait for my morning ritual of filling their bowls. I called them "The Ladies of the Club." I had names for them all—Betty, Twila, Fern, Elaine, Doris, Virginia, Venyle, Ethel, Barbara, Thelma, and

I even called one of them Edna for my Grandma Moyes. A few hummingbirds were buzzing around their feeder, and I was enjoying my morning. However, I just couldn't get "Him" out of my mind.

"Him," was my first love, Roger Couch—a man I had known and loved forty-four years earlier. Wow! Forty-four years seemed like an entire lifetime ago, a lifetime that had taken me through two divorces, the death of a husband, and having two children since I had seen him last.

The day before, I had been running errands and was in the neighborhood in downtown Phoenix where he had lived during our courtship and engagement in 1969. Yes, engagement. We became engaged on my nineteenth birthday, and for reasons we both don't seem to agree on now, broke up a short time later and went our separate ways.

I just couldn't get him off my mind that day. I had been a widow for six years and was enjoying my life to the fullest. Traveling, volunteering, and spending time with friends and family kept me busy.

I decided later that evening to see if I could find him on Facebook. So at 10:30 that night, I opened my computer and typed in Roger Couch. Guess what? Six of them. I ruled out five of them immediately, but the remaining man had a golden retriever as his profile picture. I scanned through several of his pictures, all of which had many people in skiing, biking, and snowshoeing gear. But then, there it was. A picture of him in front of his bicycle—with a full grey beard and forty-four years older. Could it really be him? It said he was living in Rigby, Idaho, and he was WIDOWED.

My heart stopped. I thought about it for a few minutes and then wrote this message: "Are you the Roger Couch I knew in Phoenix a gazillion years ago?" I waited until after midnight to get the nerve to send it.

The next morning as I opened Facebook, there it was, his reply written at 5:00 a.m.

"I couldn't believe it when I saw the name! I had to take the chance that it was you. If this is the beautiful girl, with the beautiful smile, who lived on the north end of town and whose family had a small trucking company, that I just about married, then yes, I'm that Roger Couch!"

That message took my breath away. I wrote back, "Well, that was awkward!" It had been a long time since anyone had called me beautiful.

His next message was something like, "Well, I'm not sure why you feel awkward. It's hard for me to understand what makes you feel so. It's been forty-four plus years since we have seen each other. I thought I was just stating a fact, a brief but fun or maybe interesting part of what makes us, us. I've had a great life so far, and you were a part of it. So, we can stay 'friends' or not, but it might be worthwhile sharing what's been happening since. I'm not interested in changing your life as it is, and I hope you aren't interested in changing mine. That's the beauty of Facebook. We were a part of each other's lives, so let's learn about each other since then. We don't need to change each other's lives."

Our conversations started that morning and continued

with one or two lengthy messages each day until April 25, when he said, "It's time we meet! I am coming to Salt Lake next week to buy a new guitar. Can we do dinner?" My heart stopped. Until this time, we had never even talked on the phone—just private Facebook messages.

We planned for him to come to Layton the next weekend. He told me to make reservations at any Italian restaurant I wanted, so I chose Rovali's in Ogden. He showed up at my house right on time, and as he rang the doorbell, I realized I had not even heard his voice. But there he was! Tall and just as handsome as I remembered. I don't remember too much about the drive there, but as we sat by the front window at the restaurant, talking for what seemed like hours, facing the hustle and bustle of 25th Street, we decided we were going to give what we had forty-four years ago another chance and get married.

Now the fun began—telling our family and friends and answering everyone's questions.

I called my daughter that night and said, "Boy, have I got myself into something! We need to do lunch." So, my cousin, Karen, my granddaughter, Lacey, my daughter, Michelle, and Michelle's best friend, Amy, were waiting for us as we arrived at the Union Grille in Ogden the following day. They were all wondering, "Who is this guy?"

I introduced them to Roger, told them the rest of our story, and announced we were going to get married. Keep in mind not one of them had even heard his name.

Amy: "What are your intentions?"

Michelle: "Do you need a purse or a nurse?" (A Grandma Betty favorite saying)

Lacey: "GRANDMA...?"

What went on during those next few months was definitely an adventure. Besides telling his daughter, Amanda, and my two children, there were a few added hiccups. Michelle was having heart surgery in June, and my granddaughter, Lacey, was getting married in September. My son had been working on his doctorate degree at the University of Utah and was living with me for three weeks, then going back to Phoenix for a week, repeating the pattern every month. We had planned to have his wife, Mary, and their four children, Ben, Kate, Ella, and Brixley, along with their two dogs, Happy and Lucky, come for the summer. They all arrived on the first of June.

Well, so much for "not changing each other's lives." Roger went back to Idaho, sold his house, moved to Layton, and we were married less than six months after I sent the original message.

We were married at the Historic Eccles Mansion in Ogden, Utah, on July 6, 2013. It was a beautiful ceremony with dear friends and family. There was a horrible thunderstorm just before the ceremony which made our pictures even more challenging. They had set the reception up on the outdoor patio, so immediately following the ceremony, everyone went out on the covered veranda, and the staff made some quick adjustments and prepared the inside for the dinner. Everyone laughed and had a great time. Many special memories were made that night.

For our wedding, we asked Roger's daughter, Amanda, and my son, Chad, to say a few words.

AMANDA'S TOAST:

I am Amanda, Roger's daughter. Along here with me are my husband, Scott, and our son, Ashton.

So, I have these somewhat cliché memories of my dad teaching me how to ride a bike, tie my shoes, and when I got older, how to mow the grass.

There was a rare moment when I was sixteen that I didn't hate you for ruining my life.

I remember sitting in your car with you one night listening to Fleetwood Mac for hours trying to analyze the meaning of the words to the songs. Whether or not you know it, it was moments like this that molded and defined me as a person. You are the most important person in my life.

When my mom died a couple of years ago, I was really worried about you.

Can you feed yourself?

Can you pay your bills?

Will you be lonely?

Can you be happy?

Well, with the help of great friends and your wonder dog, Charlie, you were too busy to be lonely.

But happy?

That didn't happen until you re-met Patrice.

(Lots of clapping and cheering)

Patrice, you are kind, full of spirit, and whimsy. You are what my dad needs to live a happy and full life.

Now, my dad would say he prefers predictability, but I think he needs a little occasional spontaneity, and if this wedding is any indication of that—

(Lots of laughter and clapping)

I know he is in good hands.

Patrice, you earned a spot in my heart when Ashton was having the quintessential two-year-old meltdown one day, and you just so happened to have a Hot Wheels in your purse. How can I not love a woman who is undeterred by my willful child.

And to the family, Scott and I realized that you are Ashton's first cousins. We are such a small family. So, it is amazing to be welcomed into this family, and we are looking forward to some really great memories.

CHAD'S REMARKS

as he wrote it

INTRODUCTION

My name is Chad Killebrew, and I'm the son of the bride.

Thank you all for being with us on this joyous occasion.

As many of you know, I have been living in my mom's basement during the last year while working on a PhD at the University of Utah.

One night, my mom came home with a "some guy" (point to Roger). She introduced us. Trying to make small talk, I asked, "So, Roger, what brings you to town?" He looked at my mom, and my mom raised her hand and said—with a shy smile—"Me." I chalked it up to a random experience, said it was nice to meet him, and went back downstairs to study.

The next night, my mom came to me and said, "Have a seat, we need to talk." This had happened before...several times in my youth...but this time, I was at a loss as to what I had done wrong.

She told me that a few years ago (when she was 19), she met, fell in love, and was engaged to be married to Roger. She continued, assuming that I remembered Roger's name from our introduction the day before. "Well, a few months ago, we found each other on Facebook, we've been texting and emailing, we've gone out a couple of times, he asked me to marry him, and I said, 'Yes.'" (Lots of laughter and clapping.)

I was slightly surprised; only slightly. But I did have four questions:

(1) Who's Roger?

(2) Are you pregnant? Or as Grandma Betty would say, "Are you PG?"

(3) Can I still live in your basement?

(4) What stopped the ship from sailing the first time? Why didn't they get married years ago?

She told me Roger was the man I'd met the day before. Great!

She confirmed that she was not PG.

She said I could continue to live in the basement. (What 39-year-old living away from home for weeks at a time wouldn't want to live in the basement of newlyweds? Right?)

Neither of their memories could recall the exact reason for why things didn't work out back then, but Grandpa Carl's name was mentioned a few times as a possibility. Right...Grandpa Carl "may have" had something to do with breaking up his 19-year-old daughter's engagement to a 25-year-old who had been in the Marines. I think we've identified the root cause of their earlier breakup—Carl Moyes. I'm sure Betty had an opinion on the matter as well.

So, here we are, a few years later. The environment and circumstances surrounding these two have changed over the years. But there is a common thread sewn into both the early version and this most recent version of their story—They're in love!

(Lots of clapping and cheering)

Grandpa Carl and Grandma Betty's opinions still hold tremendous sway in many of our lives. They are quoted on a daily basis in this family. So, my wife and I inquired with the heavens as to their opinion on this situation...

And then came the inspiration...through a website sponsored by Englebert Humperdink (Grandma's favorite since Mickey Gilley let her down years ago), a confirmation that B&C—Betty and Carl approve of this evening's events.

A gift was presented at this time. It was a pillowcase and a door hanger inspired by Englebert's hit, "After the lovin." A toast, to being in love!

Congratulations!

(Again, lots of clapping and laughter)

Our life has been so richly blessed. We have since sold our house in Layton to our granddaughter, Lacey, and her family, and now live in Hurricane, Utah. We love it here but do miss our families who are scattered from Utah, Idaho, Arizona, and Mexico.

CHAPTER 6

"Because I Have Been Given Much, I Too Must Give" [1]

RECENTLY, I was at a Community Preparedness Fair and came upon the Red Cross booth. Oh, the memories just started flowing.

Two nights earlier on the news, they were showing yet another hurricane in Puerto Rico and were filming from the exact city I had volunteered in twice several years ago, Toa Baja. Having seen first-hand how they suffered, I knew personally what they had gone through again.

I just cried so hard. I told Roger I loved those people, and if we were twenty years younger, we would be on an airplane to Puerto Rico.

Through my tears watching the news that night, it took me back to 1992.

The date was September 6, 1992, and I had read in the *Ogden Standard Examiner* an article asking for volunteers to go to Florida with the American Red Cross. They were interviewing David Lambert, Disaster Services Director from the local Ogden chapter. He had been to Cutler Ridge, Florida, after Hurricane Andrew struck Florida the last week of August 1992. He was explaining the urgent need for volunteers to help those who had been affected.

I was a single mom, a new grandma, and my son had just graduated from high school. I was blessed financially that I didn't need to work and felt like, being so blessed, this was something I could do. I talked to my children about it, and they said yes, I should go. It was to be a three-week assignment.

I called David Lambert that Sunday night and had a very long talk with him about this. Years later, he and his wife, who are now my dear friends, laughed about how this strange woman called him that night and wouldn't shut up!

The following Monday morning, I was in a classroom with twenty other volunteers who were ready to set sail for Miami. After a week of Intense Disaster Services, Mass Care, and Public Relations classes, I found myself on a flight with several other volunteers to Miami, September 16, 1992.

During the classes, I met Ina Sheehan, who became a very dear, lifelong friend. She and her husband, Pat, had been instructors for several years for the Red Cross and taught most of our classes that week. Ina was in the group I was traveling with, and they assigned us all to the same service center in Cutler Ridge, Florida.

After a long day of travel and hanging out at headquarters, they gave us our hotel assignment. Ina and I were going to share a room. They assigned us a hotel (using this word loosely) in North Miami. It was old and rundown. There was actually a space between the door and the doorjamb. It was also in quite a scary area. The hotels that hadn't been annihilated by the hurricane were already filled with construction workers, insurance claim adjusters, and residents who had lost their homes. This left the more undesirable and smaller hotels for those workers who came in later to work on the disaster.

On our first morning driving to the service center, we passed through forty miles of destruction. Our service center was a furniture store in the southern part of the state. It had been destroyed but was being used for that area's victims. Our daily mantra was, "When it rains in Cutler Ridge, it rains in Service Center 5."

As we parked our car and walked into the service center, we saw the line of clients waiting. There were hundreds in the line. It was ninety-five degrees and humid. These people were homeless, hungry, and mostly hopeless. These three weeks changed how I looked at desperate people. I learned patience, tolerance, and how to love the people of Cutler Ridge. They had lost everything, and most of them had no hope of any kind of future.

They took us into a room for a brief orientation and gave us our assignments and where we would sit for the next three weeks. My assignment was as a Family Service Case Worker. I interviewed the clients and assessed their emergency needs the Red Cross could assist them with and help them find other resources for what we could not provide.

As I looked out at the waiting line of over one hundred clients, I was filled with so much emotion I knew I had to talk to my children, Michelle, now age twenty-one, married, and a mother, and Chad, now eighteen. I asked my supervisor if I could be excused for a few minutes and walked to the corner where a REVCO drug store had just re-opened. I used the pay phone to call home. My daughter didn't answer. I tried my son. No answer. I tried him at his friend's house, and yes, he was there. As soon as I heard his voice, I completely broke down and cried. It scared him, and he asked what was wrong. I told him I was fine, but he just needed to let me cry it out. I told him what I was seeing and experiencing, how totally desperate these people were, and explained the total destruction of the area.

One morning, one of my clients had her little girl with her. The little girl was kind of irritable, so I gave her a pad of post-it notes and told her to draw some pictures. She drew a circle, added some eyes, a nose, a mouth, and curly hair around the circle. Then, she just started poking dots all over the face. I said "Crystal, who is that?" She said, "It is you." I said, "What is that all over my face?" She replied, "Sweat!" Yes, she was right!

I learned to love these clients, even though every once in a while we would get one that was trying to scam the system; however, most were genuinely in desperate need.

One of my clients wrote a poem and brought it to me the following day.

Dear friend whose face
I had never seen
Whose name I've never known
I don't know how to thank you
For the kindness you have shown.

When everything around me
seems uncertain and unclear
My thoughts are all a jumble
and my heart is full of fear.

I feel like I am sinking
And my boat is far from land
I start to think all hope is lost
Then I see your outstretched hand.

And now I know I'm not alone
In hope, my strengths renew
I find the courage to start again
through unseen friends like you.

– GWEN FLOWERS
Client at Service Center #5

On my final Sunday in Miami, I had asked my supervisor if I could go to church. The only Church of Jesus Christ of Latter-day Saints church building was several miles south in Homestead.

As I walked into the destroyed building, my heart broke again. Most of the military residents of the area had been relocated or moved. There were less than one hundred people at church. I had to smile at the children's clothing—all new because this area had been destroyed. They had lost everything.

After the Sacrament meeting, the ladies went into a small room with a large conference table and sat around it. There were fifteen ladies and three Red Cross Volunteers, including me. They expressed their love and gratitude to us for taking our time and efforts to come and help them. There were many tears shed.

I told them how I had decided to come and shared my love for the song "Because I have Been Given Much." I cried as I explained how, because of this song, I knew I needed to come.

After the beautiful lesson, The Relief Society President moved her papers from the top of the open hymn book and said, "Well, Sister Castansa, please pass around the box of tissues because our closing song this afternoon is 'Because I have Been Given Much.'" I get tears in my eyes even today when I think of that day.

After coming home, I was hooked on service. I became a full-time volunteer working at the local Red Cross chapter, sometimes up to four days a week.

The following year, I went to St. Louis to help with the Midwest Floods of 1993. My assignment was to work in West Alton, Missouri. The levee broke there on July 3, and most of this small farming community had to evacuate during the night. I got there the third week of September. They were just being allowed back into their town, neighborhoods, and homes. There was total destruction. It looked like a war zone. A few days after the levee broke, a tornado passed through the town, causing even more destruction. It was horrible—inches of dried, caked mud, cemeteries with head stones washed away, baby shoes and clothing hanging from the trees. It broke my heart.

Two of my first clients were Ralph and Lola Shampine. She sat across from me, and he was at the end of the table near me. He was sitting quietly with his arms folded. She was answering all my questions regarding their damage, and I was explaining how we could help them with their emergency needs.

She said they had just celebrated their fiftieth anniversary. I reached over and gave him a little nudge, and, grinning, I said, "Wow, you must be a hot number for her to put up with you all those years!" He laughed and then started talking to me. Within a few minutes, we were all laughing and sharing pictures of our grandkids. The Public Relations team was there from headquarters. They started filming us. Everyone was laughing and having a great time. Ralph got up to use the restroom, and I looked at Lola. She was crying so hard. I reached over and took her hand and asked her what was wrong. She said, "You are the first person he has talked to since we left our home over two months ago. I have my Ralph back!" We cried together that afternoon. I continued a longtime friendship with them until they both passed away.

Over the next five years, I worked on eight different national disasters, several in Puerto Rico and twice in St. John in the Virgin Islands.

In our local office, I worked in Disaster Services and also the Utility Assistance Program. I loved the clients who I worked with. One day, I was late for a nail appointment because I had seen a client walking with groceries and stopped to give her a ride home. When I got to the appointment and explained why I was late, the lady took my hand and said to me, "Patrice, the job is taken." I looked at her and wondered what she meant. Still holding my hand, she said, "The world already has a Savior! You can't save everyone."

By this time, I had received several American Red Cross awards, including the Clara Barton Award. This award is the highest recognition for volunteers and is awarded to remarkable volunteers for their service in several leadership positions. I had also taken more training and now was a Family Service Coordinator, which is a supervisor over the service centers I was assigned to on national disasters. I was also on the board of directors for the local chapter and was very active in fundraising for the chapter.

During this time, we had been through a couple of different executive directors, and we had just recently hired a new woman from Pennsylvania. I was excited for new changes and the fresh air she was bringing to the chapter after having an executive director who really had not been a good fit for the Ogden area.

Several months later, during a board meeting, the treasurer handed out the financial reports, and I noticed a huge amount this new director had submitted for her moving expenses. I had been on the selection committee that hired her, and I knew the amount that had been agreed on for her moving expenses. This exceeded that amount by over $20,000. When I saw this, my eyes met hers, and she knew I knew. The other two men who had been on the selection committee were no longer with the chapter, so I was the only one who would have known this.

No words were exchanged between us, but for the next couple of weeks, she did everything she could to get rid of me.

There had been a flood in a nearby town, Riverdale, that I had been working on. One day, I got a letter in the mail from the American Red Cross that I had been "fired." Yes, apparently you can fire a volunteer. The letter said I had told a family the chapter would replace their furnace that had been destroyed in the flood.

I never would have said that, and, in fact, told the families I helped that the Red Cross did not replace furnaces and gave them all other resources to follow up with.

When I asked her to confirm where she had got this information, she gave me the name of the family. This family, however, was a dear friend's relative. They went before the board and told them I never told them they would get a furnace and exactly what I had said and the other resources I had given them.

Over the next few weeks, it became intolerable for me as well as several other volunteers. I was accused of several things, but because of my love for what I did and the people I served, I decided I would keep quiet and not report this to anyone. I knew if I reported this, the chapter would have suffered. It was possible we could have lost funding from our major donor, who furnished us with our building. I left quietly, my heart broken and yet so angry.

But, as the saying goes, when one door closes, another one opens, and that is exactly what happened.

CHAPTER 7

As you grow older, you will discover that you have two hands—one for helping yourself, the other for helping others.

— Sam Levenson, *In One Era and out the Other*

It was about this time Richard Paul Evans, the author of a little book called *The Christmas Box*, had become somewhat of a local celebrity. Dear friends, Fred and Linda Stettler, gave me a copy of the book for Christmas in 1993, and I read it every year.

He appeared to be everywhere and had just written another little book called *The Christmas Candle*. I was at an event in Salt Lake City and came around the corner, and there HE was at a table selling HIS books. I told my daughter I wanted to get one, and wow, he will even autograph it!

While we were waiting in line, we started talking to a lady who was with him, Judy Bangerter. Judy was the Development Director at Christmas Box International. We immediately became fast friends, and my daughter began telling her about this fundraiser, "Let's Do Holiday Lunch," we had been doing for the American Red Cross for three years, but we weren't going to do it for them after this year. Judy put her arm around me and said, "I want YOU!" My daughter laughed and said, "You can't have her. She's my mom!"

That started my life with Christmas Box International. Almost twenty-five years later, my love for this organization is as strong as it was from Day One.

In 2003, my brother, Jerry, was helpful in securing the land for the Ogden Christmas Box House. The Christmas Box houses are shelter situations for children who have been taken from their homes and need a safe place until they can be placed back with their family or in foster care. I was there for the initial groundbreaking, and this year, 2023, they celebrate twenty years in Ogden. I served on the Board of Directors for several years, organized over twenty years of "Let's Do Holiday Lunch," and now am serving as a Christmas Box Resource Coordinator in St. George and Cedar City, Utah.

To see children removed from their homes through no choice of their own, be taken into the Christmas Box House is indeed a heartwarming scene. They are met by a large seasonal Christmas tree and staff who will love and protect them while they are there.

For several years, I, along with the volunteer Christmas Club ladies and my daughter, Michelle, hosted "UnBirthday Birthday Parties" each month. Every child who was in the house would get to celebrate like it was their own birthday and receive a gift. Several of the children had never had a birthday party, let alone ever received a birthday present of their very own to keep.

Through the years, it has been so heartwarming to meet some children who had lived at The Christmas Box House. Now grown, some of the young adults return to speak at the "Let's Do Holiday Lunch" and other community events about their time at the House. It is gratifying to know in some small way, through our fundraising efforts, we helped to play a part in their experience there.

My love for this organization, the staff, Richard Paul Evans, and his sweet wife, Keri, has never wavered.

CHAPTER 8

> *Good friends help you to find important things when you have lost them... Your smile, your hope and your courage.*
>
> – Doe Zantamata, *Facebook*, January 27, 2012

In the summer of 1992, my brother, Jerry, bought a new houseboat, the *Getaway 2*. It was not just any houseboat but the largest on Lake Powell at the time. It was beautiful.

The following year, a group of my girlfriends and I traveled to Page, Arizona, to spend a fun, sun-filled week on the *Getaway 2*. This started the Annual Lake Powell Girls' Trip. This year, 2023, will be our thirtieth year.

In 2000, another new boat hit the lake, *The Big Dog*. It was the largest on the lake at that time, and the boat we now get to use every year. Eventually, my daughter and her friends, then even my granddaughter and her friends, joined in. One rule they have all learned through the years is, "You have to learn to roll with the flow!" Sometimes the boat wasn't ready when we all arrived, and sometimes the boat wasn't even there for us.

In deciding each year who to invite, I would ask myself, "WHO needs this trip?" Several of the women had never been to Lake Powell and, for some, had never been on a vacation by themselves. By the second year, we had called ourselves the "Displaced Homemakers Association," and the only criteria was to have divorced at least once or have thought of it once. We thought we were pretty clever. What started as a group of about twenty friends grew over the next thirty years to include over one hundred friends and family. Some brought daughters, and even a mom or grandma got to come along. One year, we even had a brand-new baby join us with her new mommy.

For several years, we would have our Annual Talent Night. Sometimes, these words were used very loosely. There were several groups of friends who would get together and plan their best. We had everything: hula dancing, several lip-syncing specialties, invisible baton routines to "The Stars and Stripes Forever," and one year a group of fourteen in decorated bras singing loudly and proudly to The Saliva Sisters, "Brahide." One group took some of us more "mature" ladies' swimming suits, stuffed them in certain areas, and did a synchronized swimming routine that brought the house down in laughter. Once, one group made a movie called "Jerry's Angels!" One year, I even did a double baton routine on the upper deck of the boat at sunset and didn't drop either one! In 2002, we had the Lake Powell Olympics with various water and hilarious beach events. This last year, fifteen of the ladies dressed in blow-up black and white cow costumes and surprised the others to a dance to Lizzo's "It's About Damn Time."

Some have come every year, and others have decided it just wasn't for them. Some love the sun, but others not so much. Some play cards, some sew, some knit and crochet. Some drink and, well, drink some more. Some water ski, some love the wave runners.

We have celebrated births, deaths of parents, spouses, children and grandchildren. We have seen each other through divorces, marriages, hardships, and celebrations. We have had bridal showers, a fertility ceremony, memorial services for lost friends, and last year, we scattered ashes of a loved one in a private cove.

There have been so many friendships and bonding throughout the years, and each year we try to remember the friends we have lost. The following words written by a dear friend, Jeanne Young, in 2003 can sum up the entire experience pretty well.

The Big Dog Gift

You come here for the week away
You come here for the sun and the water and the beaches.
You come here knowing that you'll drink too much,
laugh too loud, party too hard, and eat too much.
And for the most part, that's ok because the number
one rule is, "What happens here, stays here."
You come here knowing that most of the regulars will be here,
and you come knowing you'll meet many newcomers.

You come here with too much luggage
but not enough outfits.
You save up all your goofy gags and jokes to share
with a very appreciative but captive audience.
You sign up for cooking and cleaning,
and you actually enjoy it.
You agree cheerfully to domestic stuff you'd never
consider in the life you put on pause while you're here.
Initially, you sort and catagorize all these women,
mostly tall, blonde, and thin.
And you hate 'em all.
But then, you take another look,
they're not all tall, they're not all blonde,
and they're not all thin!
And as time goes on,
you find that some are really kind and sweet,
a few are terribly funny,
and most have the same insecurities
and self doubts you have.
And it's OK.
You are in the company of some great women.
Everything they told you about this week is true.
Everything about this week is good,
and then there is a little surprise.
These women encourage each other,
and they support each other.

And for a few days they help you find
your way back, back to the best you.
How old were you when you forgot
how young and beautiful you once were?
How old are you when you can't remember
that you were strong and golden in the sun?
What year did you resign your youth,
not even knowing that you did it?
Everything and everybody here helps you see that
time when you were young and beautiful and strong.
You come here for all the wrong reasons,
but you leave with all the right results.

A dear friend recently asked me, "What have YOU got out of these trips?" Yes, they are a lot of work: planning sleeping arrangements, food for eighteen meals, entertainment, transportation, and trying to keep everyone safe and everything running on a seventy-eight-foot houseboat.

I think the experience of just knowing everyone is having a great time, experiencing something that many never have had the chance to, and having fun myself is enough. My friend wrote, "You have given so much and provided a great experience for many friends, friends and acquaintances of friends and family, with most of the time receiving little in return; but it's an experience that affected every woman that has had the opportunity one way or another with a ton of gratitude from most all, certainly myself included." And that is enough for me.

As each year comes and goes and we tell each other goodbye, we all realize it might be the last year for some, and so, we value the friendships made and look forward to the next year. We have been truly blessed by my brother's generosity in allowing us to continue this awesome tradition and fun.

From this fabulous group of friends, another fun tradition was started. In 1994, when we were all getting ready to leave the boat, we were talking about when to get together next. We decided to get together for lunch during the holidays. That year, about twenty of us high school friends got together and talked about how to do this each year.

I was heavily involved with the American Red Cross and knew the Disaster Services of the chapter needed some fundraising. My dear friend, Dee Ladd, suggested we do a holiday lunch and call it "Let's Do Holiday Lunch." The idea was everyone always says, "Let's get together during the holidays for lunch," or bosses take employees out. Why not make some money and have fun at the same time? And that is how "Let's Do Holiday Lunch" was born.

The first year, we had eighty in attendance. We had a fashion show with clothing from Northern Reflections. Several friends, a few employees, and even my mother were our models. We had a few silent auction items we had put together along with several camp quilts a dear friend had also donated. We made $3,000 and were so excited.

When my friend suggested the name for the event, she also strongly suggested I register the name with the state, so I could always be in control of the event. We continued to have it two more years for the American Red Cross but changed over to the Christmas Box International in 1998.

This was always such a fun event after we made the switch because we could always have Richard Paul Evans as the speaker. He had become a local celebrity by this time, so besides having a fun event, we were treated to his inspirational words. He always made us cry.

We would sell out almost every year for this luncheon. Something everyone loved about it was our silent auction items. We tried really hard to have something everyone could afford to bid on. My committee in the beginning was my daughter and her best friend, Amy. We would assemble the baskets in my basement and transport them to the event. In 2007, Jeff died the week of the luncheon. My dear friend, Darlene Thatcher, had volunteered earlier in the year to use her basement to assemble them, not having any idea what was ahead of us for that week. This was indeed a true blessing. My friends and neighbors all came together that week at her home and created miracles. As the event grew, eventually the Christmas Club, a group of wonderful volunteers at the Ogden Christmas Box House, also started helping.

One year, we assembled the baskets in a freezing warehouse with extension cords from one of the other units to keep some heaters going. The ground was frozen, but we kept popping out the baskets. As we were cleaning up after the event, Larene Jaques, Amy's mom, told us we could use her old house she had recently moved from to house our inventories. We could use it all year for just "Let's Do Holiday Lunch." This was such a blessing. As items were gathered and donated, we could take them to the house where we had tables and shelves and heat.

My mother was usually in Phoenix during this time of year, so every year, my brother, Jerry, would fly her and all her friends up for the luncheon, which was always the kickoff for the holiday season. There were so many friends and family who supported this luncheon over the years, and everyone looked forward to seeing old friends we knew would always be there.

In the early days, we never really had a bookkeeper; we just turned the monies over to The Christmas Box. I never really knew how much money was made through the years but have heard it was over $300,000.00.

In 2016, Roger and I moved to Hurricane, Utah, permanently. That was my last year hosting the event. The following year, I asked Kearston Cutrubus, who had been an awesome supporter of the luncheon and served on the Board of Directors of Christmas Box International, if she would like to take on the event. She agreed and it still continues to be a fun Christmas event in Ogden.

In 2021, a nonprofit in St. George, Memory Matters, asked if I would consider doing the luncheon for them. I told them no, I wasn't interested. My friend, Kim Boyer, asked me again and then again, so I told her I would think about it. I wanted to come to one of their board meetings and see what their organization was all about. I had never heard of them prior to that time. As I walked into their humble office, I met the director, LuAnn Lundquist, and her husband, Kurt, and a few of the other board members. I looked through a window into a room where their clients were doing some arts and crafts, gluing pom-poms on paper, and coloring. In another room, a group was singing, "I've Been Working on the Railroad." I was hooked! Dementia and memory loss clients stole my heart. So now there is a "Let's Do Holiday Lunch" in St. George and Ogden, Utah. Both are successful events, and both are for organizations that are so dear to me. I am so thankful to be a part of both.

CHAPTER 9

A tithket, a tathket....
(A tisket, a tasket)

In 1960, I was in the fourth grade. One day, the most beautiful woman I had ever seen came into our classroom. She went to the back of the classroom to talk to the teacher, Mr. Wiser. I heard him say, "Yes, Patrice Moyes. Patrice, will you please come here?"

I thought this was the luckiest day in my life. I was going to get to go with this beautiful lady.

Little did I know she was the Weber County School Speech Therapist. I followed her into a little room by the principal's office.

Apparently, I had a terrible speech problem that, until then, no one had mentioned to me, and I couldn't hear it myself.

As she introduced herself to me, she explained what was going to happen in the therapy classes. She had a huge reel-to-reel tape recorder and said she was going to record me reciting different poems and then play them back to me. I thought that was harmless.

"Seven little sailers, sailed the seven seas..."

I finished the poem, and she pushed replay.

I was crushed, shocked, humiliated, and totally scared at what I was hearing. I cried and cried and said that couldn't be me talking. After she calmed me down, she explained to me we never sound to ourselves as others hear us. She explained I had what was called a bilateral lisp, and she was going to do everything she could to help me overcome it.

My s's, ch's, sl's were mushy. I cried the rest of the day and asked if I could walk home. When I told my mom what had happened, she went back to the school with me, and we and the speech therapist talked over the plan to help me with my speech.

I eventually learned to get over the lisp by placing a wooden skewer between my front teeth and repeat the poem "Seven little sailers" over and over for what I can remember was months.

I still struggle all these years later with some of those sounds.

As if the problem with my speech wasn't enough, it got worse. In 2014, we bought a house in Hurricane, Utah, and shared our time between there and our home in Layton.

January 25, 2015, was just another beautiful, sunny day. I had been struggling with an issue with a friend and had been crying most of the night. I got up, started eating a bowl of oatmeal, and realized my mouth was numb as the oatmeal spilled down my chin.

I yelled for Roger. We thought I was having a stroke, and he drove me immediately to the Hurricane Clinic. They sent me from there to the St. George Intermountain Hospital, still thinking I was possibly having a stroke, but the nurse mentioned Bell's Palsy could be a possibility as well.

After testing and a CAT scan at the hospital, they ruled out a stroke and sent me home. They diagnosed me with nausea and instructed me to follow up with my primary care doctor if it didn't get better. By the time we got home, the right side of my face was completely drooped, completely numb, and so very painful. I couldn't close my eye and couldn't smile. It was the most horrible, frightening, and saddest day of my life!

It was Bell's Palsy. The following Monday, I went to my doctor and received cortisone and antiviral medication. The doctor stated they really didn't know what caused it and don't know how long it will last. I would soak in my bathtub every night and go through exhausting facial exercises, while no one could see me.

Months went by with no improvement. The pain could be excruciating, as well as the embarrassment of my droopy face and smile. After several months, I could get my eye closed, and my smile started to come back. I am still not back 100 percent, and every few months, I get shots on the side of my eye to keep it open. I am so grateful, however, for the progress and improvement I made.

Not once, through any of this illness, did Roger's love for my beautiful, crooked smile waver.

CHAPTER 10

If today gets difficult, remember the smell of coffee, the way sunlight bounces off a window, the sound of your favorite person's laugh, the feeling when a song you love comes on, the color of the sky at dusk, and that we are all here to take care of each other.

– Nanea Hoffman, *Instagram*, May 3, 2022

In May 2007, I had the opportunity to travel with my dear friend, Ina Sheehan, and several others on a medical mission to Timisoara, Romania. This was an amazing trip where I met Pastor Peter Dugulescu, his lovely wife, Mary, and their daughter, Ligia.

Ina had gone the previous year on this medical mission and was preparing to go again. I asked her if she thought they would allow me to go since I wasn't a member of the church sponsoring it, Washington Heights Baptist Church in Ogden, Utah. She said she would ask. I waited patiently for over a week, then she called me and told me I would need to meet with the leader of the group, Sam Barber, for an interview.

He told me yes, I could go, but I needed to be "thick skinned" and prepared for other's views and values because no one else on the trip believed in the "Mormon" faith. I agreed and told him yes, I understood.

It was an amazing trip. The name of the organization we were there helping was Jesus, Hope of Romania. This was another three-week experience that changed me yet again on how I looked at others' beliefs, traditions, and ways of life.

Again, this was a time in my life where angels were around me.

My assignment was to help fit the clients with eyeglasses. Hundreds of donated eyeglasses were sent ahead, so when we got there, we just had to sort them.

I had a young man, Alex, who had been working with me as an interpreter. He was seventeen, the same age as my granddaughter, Lacey. He was living at the Onemisus House, a home for children who had been abandoned by parents, street children, or any child needing a home.

I asked him how he came to live there, and he said his parents had given him up during the revolution, and gypsies had taken him in. The gypsies made him steal, and eventually, he was placed at the Onemisus House.

Revolution? 1989? Living in Utah, I did not know in December 1989, an obsolete and inhumane communist system was crumbling under the weight of its own lies. Crowds of over 150,000 gathered in the square in Timisoura for several days until official word came that the dictator Ceausescu had been overthrown. When the crowds heard the news, the people shouted enthusiastically, "God Exists! God Exists!"

It was on this day Pastor Peter Dugulescu was addressing the crowd from the balcony of the Opera House at the opposite end of the square to the cathedral. When he invited the crowd to recite after him the Lord's Prayer, they instinctively turned to face the cathedral, kneeling on the frozen ground.

Within two days, the revolution had spread across the country. The dictator and his wife had to flee in a helicopter, only to be arrested, tried, and executed. A handful of brave, faithful Christian church members standing in solidarity with their pastor had triggered an improbable revolution. I am so proud to have met Pastor Dugulescu and his sweet wife, Mary. Peter had a massive heart attack a year after we were there and passed away.

What makes this such a bittersweet story for me is I remember hearing the story of him on the balcony of the Opera House leading the people in the Lord's Prayer. One night while we were in Timisoura, we had the opportunity to go to the opera, *La Boheme*. It was so hot I had to leave and went out onto the balcony. As I looked over the square and down the street to the beautiful cathedral in front of me, I became very emotional, picturing 150,000 people in this square, facing the cathedral, being led by Peter, kneeling on frozen ground repeating the Lord's Prayer.

The people we were there helping were all so humble. One day, a sweet little lady clothed in heavy, layered clothing was hoping to get some glasses. She told Alex what she wanted them for. Usually, when they would put a pair on, they would pick up their Bible and see if it helped them to see better to read. This woman put a pair on, turned her coat collar over to check something, shook her finger at me, and would say NO! NO!! We tried another pair, and she would do the same thing. She wasn't checking her Bible, she was looking at something on her collar. Finally! We found the pair. As she turned her collar over to check, she started crying and laughing and praising God. I asked Alex what she was looking at. He told me she had a needle stuck in the collar of her coat, and all she wanted was to thread her needle. Oh, the simplest of things we take so for granted!

I am still in contact with Alex. He is a remarkable young man living in Germany with his wife and daughter.

As we were leaving Romania, a few of us were going to be continuing on to Austria. We had to be very careful packing our luggage because of weight. As we were in the waiting area at Timisoura airport before our flight, I thought I heard my name called over the intercom. I went to tell Sam, our director, I had just heard my name being paged.

He was very nervous as we walked over to the desk. Yes, it was my name. They took us into a very small room. As we walked in, there were two HEAVILY armed guards, and there on a table was my suitcase. They motioned, very sternly, for me to open it. As I did, I realized what they were looking at. On top of everything in my suitcase was a small box of AA batteries we had been told to bring. To the side of this was my insulated mug, and to the side of that was my curling iron with the cord weaving across all of this. Sam and I breathed our sighs of relief, but the guards were not amused. They muttered for me to close my bag and LEAVE!

During the three weeks I was in Romania, we had been in areas where we had no communication with home.

When I got home, Jeff had written this poem. (Punctuation is as written!)

Alone, so alone
Alone now that you are far away
Now, nothing being said between us
The telephone so silent it screams at me.
Why won't she call I want to scream back.
I worry so
Are you well
Have the Romanians captured you
Made you a hostage
A mistaken drug trafficker
International intrique
News at six and again at ten.
Radical Baptists and one Mormon captured in Romania
More on this story following the Weather
Is there bail for hardened Baptist criminals and one
    token Mormon?
Imagination often borders insanity
Makes Romania a dismal far away prison
For American do-gooders
Shave their heads

Take away their cell phone
Panic, now…how would I know,
how could I know.
Would the embassy call
Send an Email
At least then I'd know
Could go on television
Make a plea
Enlist public support
Raid Romania
Send in Special Forces
Cease Bucharest
Threaten to drop the bomb
Put 'em in their place to
Get YOU back again!
But Romania is just Romania
No worse than California
Probably quite more civilized
Just busy, that's it…you're busy
Too busy to know of my concern for you
I don't worry though
No God even in his finest hour of taking
Would take you away from me
He knows…
He knows of our love
Our love for one another.
And he loves Baptist criminals
And one token Mormon

You do what you are meant to do
And I'll wait
But still…I am alone
Just me and my imagination.

– Jeff Archibald, May 2007

In the spring of 2009, dear Ina asked me to go on an Alaskan cruise with her. After I agreed to go, she told me we would need to get travel insurance because her doctors had recently diagnosed her with pancreatic cancer. Her doctor said she might not live longer than those few months prior to the cruise. She beat those odds and made it and several more months before she passed away.

One night on the cruise, we pretended to be journalists from our local newspaper and would find interesting people and ask them if we could interview them. We had so much fun and met so many fun fellow travelers.

Oh, we had so much fun on that trip. Memories of my dear friend still bring tears to my eyes.

As Ina was approaching her final days, she called me one morning and asked me to come over to her home. When I got there, she had a few treasures she wanted me to have. One was a one-piece girdle she had worn during one of our Lake Powell Girls' Trip talents. She asked me to take it every year and hang it in a prominent spot, so she could be there with us. She then asked me if I would speak at her funeral. I was so honored. She said, "Only about five minutes because there will be other speakers as well."

I had my five minutes prepared. The night before her funeral, her son called me and asked if I was ready to speak. He told me I had about fifteen minutes. I told him SHE had only given me five minutes. He laughed and said, "Oh, no, you are our main speaker." It didn't take me long at all to fill that extra ten minutes. I talked about the many hats she wore during her life. She was an educator, a social worker, a volunteer, and a dear friend, but her favorite hat of all to wear was the Matriarch of the Lake Powell Girls' Trip. She was older than most of us, and she would take all year experimenting on fun, different cocktails to share with those who were willing to try them.

Oh, I miss her.

CHAPTER 11

Oh, the places you go...

THEY SAY YOU LEARN FAST who does and does not make good travel partners. I have been blessed to have traveled with the best. For my sixtieth birthday, my daughter, Michelle, wrote a poem for me and called it "Where in the World is Grandma Patrice?" I have, in fact, been everywhere she mentioned except Unkenberg!

Where in the World is Grandma Patrice?

We have the best grandma in the world
To us there's no one kinder.
But if we want some Grandma time,
First we need to find her.
Where do we start? We need a plan
To find Grandma with ease.
A map? A globe? The internet?
How about our ABC's?

"A" is for Anthem, Arizona
Sometimes we find her there.
But she's also been to Austria, Atlanta
and Alaska (twice in the same year).

"B" is for such places as Beaver and Boise.
And for a town called Bonn, that's in Germany!

For "C" we'll check Chicago,
She could be there now.
But then she could be snorkeling
in Cancun or Curaçao.

The Dominican Republic would be a
good place to start for "D"
Next we could try Denver, Dallas
and then maybe Deer Valley.

"E" of course for Edmonton
She's always by a mall.
Maybe in Ely or Evanston
We really wish she'd call.

"F" we'll look in Florida,
Flagstaff or Farr West
Where her daughter, Michelle lives
(She really loves her best).

For "G" we'll try looking in Geneva—or Grover

"H" will send us looking in Hawaii—or even Hanover.

"I" is for Idaho
to see her Aunt Sally
But we're pretty sure she's gone back
To her favorite, Italy.

"J" might find her in Jackson Hole
or maybe in New Jersey

"K" could find her in Kanab
or even in Kentucky.

"L" possibly could find her
In Lake Powell or in L.A.
But Grandma's house in Layton
Is where we wish she'd stay.

"M" could find her having tea
With Martina in Maryland
Or maybe in Missouri
lending a helping hand.

"N" could find her with Paula
On the New York shopping scenes
In Naples? Nogales? or Nephi?
Or catching beads in New Orleans?

"O" let's look in Ogden
For Grandma cruising down the 'vard
From Oakland to Orlando
Maybe she'll send us a postcard.

"P" is here for Phoenix
Palm Springs and for Perth
But mostly it's for Plain City
The greatest hometown on earth!

The next one may be a little hard
Not many "Q"s in sight.
I guess we could look in Queens, New York
Or out west in old Quartzite?

For "R" we'll look in Rupert
Or perhaps Rancho Del Rey
Maybe she's in Romania
with her good friend Ina Mae?

"S" could find her in Salzburg
Or in San Fran getting her groove on
Or downtown Salt Lake with cousin Karen
Running the marathon.

"T" is for Tallahassee,
Tijuana, and Times Square
Lake Tahoe and for Tulsa
Whew! She's been everywhere!

For "U" we'll look in Unkenberg
In a quaint little chalet
Or wait patiently for our souvenirs
in Utah, USA!

We think for “V” she was spotted
Headed to Vail on the “Redeye”
But we’ve also had reports from Venice
And the Palace of Versailles.

For “W” we’ll look in Wendover
Where she goes with her aunts to play
I’ll be looking in Walla Walla
Just because it’s fun to say!

I think the map is broken
It keeps saying “X” marks the spot
But after all our searching
Still, our Grandma we have not!

“Y” is almost at the end
It’s been like chasing a cyclone
Only a few more places to search
Yuma, then Yellowstone!

So now we’ve searched from “A” to “Z”
For our dear Matriarch
The only place left to look
Is in Zion’s National Park.

Although it’s sometimes sad
When we are all apart
We always know that Grandma
Takes us with her in her heart!

It seems like turning sixty turned me into a true world traveler. I traveled to Alaska on the beautiful Polar Express, a one-hundred-foot personal yacht owned by Aleide and Dick Bennett. I am fortunate enough to be a dear friend of their daughter, Amy, and was invited three different years on this expedition.

Continuing my 60th birthday celebrations, May 2010 also found me in Paris with dear friends, Martina Hastings, Nancy Brandon, and Gwen Marable. Martina and I had met several years earlier at an art convention. We immediately hit it off, even though we were so very different. She was a psychiatric nurse, lived in Baltimore, Maryland, very political, had different beliefs in our higher power, and had been a real-life hippie. My favorite story of her hippie days was when she and her two friends drove across Mexico in an old ice cream truck. We loved each other. I told her I would travel anywhere with her, but she needed to plan it.

Before I knew it, she had our plane reservations made, our apartment rented, and the four of us were off to Paris for two weeks. They say if you have an apartment in Paris, you can actually say that you "lived" in Paris. So, the four of us lived in Paris. When we came home, I just wasn't sure what to write in my journal about the trip, so I wrote:

Things I did, ate, and saw in Paris May 2010

- I saw a mamma pigeon feeding her baby on top of a doorway leading into an old courtyard.
- I paid 100 euro to eat a quail egg and watercress soup—yuck!
- I watched the locks change in the canal in the middle of Paris.
- I rode a Segway through the Tuilleries Garden, around the Eiffel Tower, and through the streets of Paris.
- I tried on a dress in a HOT two-foot-by-two-foot dressing room with no door. Yes, I bought it and have never worn it!
- I fed large doves in Luxemburg Garden.
- I witnessed pompous, arrogant Orthodox Jewish men.
- I watched a young French man climb in my bedroom window and actually paid him 100 euro to do it! (We had locked ourselves out of our apartment which had our packed suitcases in it just a few hours before we were to leave for the airport to come home.)

- I attended an International Mass at the Notre Dame Cathedral.
- I feared for my life one night.
- I ate falafel.
- I ate a lot of bad food.
- I ate and smelled the worse cheese ever.
- I walked through several castles.
- I saw a swan in her nest.
- I saw a true wine cellar.
- I was at the live Lido.
- I walked down the Champs-Elysees.
- I spent a lot of money.
- I LIVED in Paris.
- I did my first sketch in the oldest church in Paris.
- I bought and ACTUALLY wore a purple beret.
- I ordered many meals in really bad French.
- I met an Adam Lambert look alike. I still think it was really him!
- I rode a funiculare.

- I walked along the Seine.
- I strolled along the shortest river in Europe.
- I spent a day and night with a charming family in the French countryside.
- I had the best ham and cheese sandwich EVER!
- I had lunch in the Executive Dining Room at Enesco, with a beautiful view of the Eiffel Tower.
- I ventured out by myself, doing the Metro, Open Air bus, and home again besides I know, walking at least an entire marathon that same day.
- I saw lots of romance.

It was a magical trip, one I will cherish forever.

Martina recently passed away. Another friend gone way too soon.

CHAPTER 12

So, what if, instead of thinking about solving your whole life, you just think about adding additional good things. One at a time. Just let your pile of good things grow.

– Rainbow Rowell, *Attachments: A Novel*

Again, for not changing each other's lives, as Roger said in his first message to me, we have been on some fun adventures over the years—sightseeing in Nauvoo and Palmyra, finding my old apartment in Paris, cruising the Rhine River Valley in Germany, fishing in Alaska and Mexico, and many places in between.

In 2014, we rode our Harley Davidson over 1,700 miles to Sturgis, South Dakota, with friends. We also bought an Arctic Cat Wildcat 1000 side-by-side. Everyone, it seemed, in Southern Utah had one. Roger's Idaho friends said he had gone to the "dark side" because he was an avid hiker and bicyclist when he lived there, and side-by-sides were not held in high favor by them.

In August 2017, Roger and I traveled to Puebla, Mexico, on a medical mission with my brother, Jerry, Michael Nebeker, and several others to witness surgeries be performed on children with cleft lip deformities. Jerry and Michael were there to formulate a plan on how to bring a mobile surgery hospital to Mexico. This consists of three semitrailers that were transformed into three different surgery units that can be transported throughout the country.

One morning, Roger and I were allowed to witness separate surgeries on two children. What sweet little spirits they were. One little boy, Christian, was adorable. I could have stolen him and brought him home with me. The little girl Roger was in surgery with, Alison, was a precious little nine-month-old with a cleft lip and palate. The morning after the surgeries, we went to the patients' release area and found Alison and her mom. Her mother was feeding her by actually dripping milk from the nipple of the bottle into her mouth. Because of her surgery, Alison could not suck but could swallow. Roger asked if he could help. I have a tender video of him standing over this sweet child, dripping liquid from her bottle into her tiny, bandaged mouth, with her looking directly into his eyes.

Our biggest heartbreak was watching them walk out of the hospital, knowing for most of them, they would have to travel by bus for long hours to return to their homes. A few months after we were there, they had a powerful earthquake in Puebla, and we often wondered what happened to our sweet Christian and Alison.

As we were leaving to fly home, I asked Michael why Roger and I were permitted to wear scrubs and witness two actual surgeries. He said, "Well, we told them you were major donors." I had told Michael previously Roger and I wanted to help and asked for his suggestions. He said they wanted to have every child that had surgery to have their own blanket to take home with them. So, 5000 Blankets for Smiles was created. As of this date, many friends, church groups, and family have sent over 950 blankets to Mexico for the children having surgery.

One of our most memorable trips was in May 2020. On my seventieth birthday, we decided to buy a motorhome. We had some fun adventures. In July 2021, we set out from Ogden with two other couples in their motorhomes and started a thirty-day trip to Oshkosh, Wisconsin, to the EAA Air Show.

My friend from kindergarten, Judy Hunter Cottam, planned the entire trip, and all we did was follow along. She and her husband, Larry, and the other couple, Dave and D.J. Kiehl, were all seasoned "motorhomers." We had so much fun along the way seeing all the sights Judy had planned out for us.

Several sights were amazing, but one of my favorites was the Enchanted Highway, a collection of the world's largest scrap metal sculptures constructed by Gary Greff. These are placed along a thirty-two-mile stretch of a two-lane highway in the southwestern part of North Dakota. As we entered the small town of Regent, North Dakota, there were only a few small businesses along the street. One looked like a little ice cream shop. We all decided we needed a break, so we went inside. There was a man scooping the ice cream and helping the various other customers. After talking with him briefly, we realized he was Gary Greff, the sculptor who had created these fun, enormous sculptures. Roger and I bought two of the small yard art replicas of the original huge pieces placed out on the highway and enjoy looking at them every day.

On the final night of our vacation, we were in Omro, Wisconsin, July 29, 2021. We were packed and ready to leave for home the next morning after being gone for thirty days. Shortly after we had gone to bed, my brother, Jerry, called to check on us and see how we were doing. While I was talking to him, I got an emergency weather alert on my phone. I told him I would have to call him back and checked the details on my phone. It showed we were in the path of a tornado for the next fifteen minutes. I hollered at Roger and called Judy, who was camped next to us, to see if she had received the same alert. Just as we were talking, her alert went off.

When we opened our front curtains, we couldn't believe what we saw. Prior to this alert on our phone, we had no warning of this weather coming our way. It was purple, flashing lightning so hard and fast the sky seemed to stay continuously illuminated. Constant! I started taking videos and called the kids and told them about our situation. There was nowhere we could go. We were at a small campground in the middle of a cornfield.

This weather continued for over an hour of constant wind, rain, and lightning. The storm created the most horrific sounds I had ever heard. Our power went out during this. After about an hour and a half, the rain was hitting our front windshield so hard. I told Roger it was so loud that it sounded like fire hoses pelting against it and I thought it was going to break. Roger, our golden retriever Sherman, and I huddled together on the couch. Suddenly, there was a horrible cracking sound, and something hit our roof. It was pitch black in the motorhome except for our phone lights. We thought the lightning had struck us. Water was leaking in through the damaged roof, but there was nothing we could do until the rain subsided, and we could get outside to assess the damage.

It was not lightning that had struck us, it was actually a huge tree limb that had broken and fallen across the top of the motorhome, hitting our air conditioner forcing it to break through the ceiling, causing extensive damage.

The next morning, we surveyed the damage. The owner of the campground came to help us remove all the debris that had landed on top of the motorhome. I just sat and cried. However, before we left the campground that morning, I asked Roger to get us two of the logs cut from the limb that hit us. One is sitting by our front door and the other is in the backyard.

The insurance adjuster told us if we could drive the motorhome, leave for home. There had been so much extensive damage from the storm she wasn't sure when, or even if, they could get an adjuster out to see us. We could drive it; however, we didn't have air conditioning. We took a week to get back to Ogden.

It took eleven months for the repairs to be made, and, in the long run, the insurance should have totaled it. The damage was more severe than the original bid estimated. We did eventually sell it after it was repaired but still keep several fun memories.

Oh, The Places You Go!

CHAPTER 13

Here's to strong women. May we know them.
May we be them. May we raise them.

UNKNOWN

AFTER ONE OF OUR VACATIONS in 2016, we had just returned home from ten days visiting various church history sites from Palmyra, New York, to Independence, Missouri. This was an awesome trip for us, meeting new friends and seeing several temples and historical sites.

The night after we returned, Roger was getting ready to go to a meeting and received an email from a lady. It said, "Dear Mr. Couch, according to Ancestry.com, you are 100 percent my father. I have been looking for you for over thirty years. I want you to know I am aware this can cause you discomfort and possible bad memories, I do not intend to cause you problems. My mother knows nothing about this and will not. I will ask your consideration and please give me one hour of your time. If you will allow that, I will ask no more of you. I truly hope to hear from you." She also sent a photo of herself.

Roger handed me the phone and said, "Wow, look at this scam!" I read it and was so shocked. She looked just like him through the eyes and had a remarkable resemblance to his daughter, Amanda.

He said it couldn't possibly be his daughter, and he sent her back a message saying so. Roger said to me, "I was married to Pam thirty years ago, and I was never unfaithful to her." Her message didn't say she was thirty, only that she had been looking for him for thirty years.

I argued with him saying, "Look at her, Roger. She has your eyes and looks so much like Amanda. What if she reaches out to Amanda?" He denied all of it and left for his meeting. I went directly to Facebook and found her. She was beautiful. It said she was born in 1967 and was now living in Yuma, Arizona.

In 1967, Roger returned from Viet Nam and was stationed in Yuma. She had to be his daughter. My first thoughts were so selfish. How is this going to affect me, my marriage, and our families?

That night after he returned from the meeting, we didn't discuss it. The following morning, I said to him I knew she was his daughter, and we needed to address it. He said yes, he had been in contact with her husband, and that yes, she was indeed his daughter. Her husband Rick had sent Roger a message explaining they were pretty sure he was her dad, Ancestry didn't make mistakes. They discussed what information they had and agreed yes, he was her father.

After he had returned to Yuma from his time in Viet Nam, on weekends he and his friends would go over the border to San Luis, Mexico, to party. There was always lots of drinking, and one weekend he spent some time with a waitress, Patricia's mother. Yes, her name is Patricia.

In Patricia's letter to Roger, she explained her mother and her other siblings were all dark hair and dark eyes, and she was blonde with blue eyes. Living in Mexico, she had always wondered why she looked different. When she was thirteen, she asked her mother about her dad. Her mother told her he was a gringo with whom she had a very short relationship, and Patricia looked just like him. She said she didn't know his name, and he did not know about her. Patricia searched for years, spending hours in the Yuma library looking for any information that might help her find him. One day, she heard about the Ancestry website and gave it a try. Roger and I had recently done the Ancestry DNA testing for fun.

She said the morning of September 15, 2016, she opened her email, and there it was—a DNA match that was 100 percent. She couldn't believe she had found her father. She later said, "It is everything I could have ever dreamed of but never dared to. I do look just like him, his blue eyes, his cheekbones, his smile, everything! Next week, I will meet him for the first time in my life. I will get to look at my dad's face, I will get to hold his hand and have him hug me. A hug for a daughter from a father."

We arranged to meet them the following week in Las

Vegas, Nevada. They were living in Yuma, so we decided this would be the best place to meet.

I spent all week putting together a scrapbook of Roger's childhood and our life together with all our families, and we took it to her. Roger bought her flowers, and as we waited outside of their hotel room, he paced like a new dad outside a newborn nursery waiting for a new baby.

The meeting was magic. Hugs, tears, and laughter filled the room.

The blessings to this new addition to our family were another four grandchildren and seven new great-grandchildren. This has indeed been a true blessing in our lives.

The following week, Roger got a message on his phone, and he came to me and said, "Well, so much for not changing each other's lives…" and we laughed and laughed! The message he received was another message from Patricia.

Because she had spent all those years looking for her father and not finding him, she had applied for US Citizenship on her own. She had just been notified she was going to receive her US Citizenship in Phoenix at the end of October.

Roger and I and some of our family went to Phoenix to witness this glorious event and afterward had the party of all parties. Cherrill Knight, a lady who was like my second mother, hosted the party. All the Knight, the Moyes, and the Couch families were together for one joyous night, something that had never happened before and will probably never happen again.

Rick and Patricia have since moved to Ensenada, Mexico. We have a new family tradition of spending Thanksgiving with them in Mexico and spending time with our grandchildren and great-grandchildren. We haven't been able to communicate well with three of the children except through smiles, laughs, and hugs because we don't know Spanish, and they don't know English. They are working on this now in their schools, so hopefully this Thanksgiving, we will be able to talk with them. They are learning but still not really confident. Me? I'm too old to learn Spanish, so I just smile a lot and give them lots of hugs!

CHAPTER 14

Begin with the end in Mind.

– Stephen R. Covey, *The 7 Habits of Highly Effective People*

In the fall of 1990, I was recently divorced for the second time. My son was a sophomore in high school. We were getting along really well, but I was missing something. I needed something that made me feel useful. Financially, I did not have to work, but still I needed something to add value to my life.

I had heard of a leadership program by Stephen R. Covey, *7 Habits of Highly Effective People*, and there was a Facilitator Training Program available. I asked my brother, Jerry, who was the president of Swift Transportation, if this was something he would be interested in and let me become a facilitator at Swift for the employees. Their new motto was, "Carrier of the 90's!" He agreed, so I applied.

It was a weeklong training session at Sundance Resort in Sundance, Utah. The morning of our orientation, we were told Stephen would not be there, he had another commitment.

We were all assembled in the resort auditorium. They instructed us to stand and introduce ourselves, identify our position at our corporations, and share what we expected to learn from this program. I panicked. Position? I didn't have a position, I didn't have a title, I didn't even have a job!

I was in the seventh row, and as everyone introduced themselves, I knew I was in trouble. They were talking about positions I had never heard of. The main one was, "I am the Director of HR." HR? What was HR? Soon my turn came, and I stood and said, "My name is Patrice Scott. I am working for Swift Transportation and hope I can add something valuable to them in what I will be learning here this week. Oh, and I am a new grandma!" My voice was quivering, and I was nervous. Just as I sat down, a hand came from behind me and patted me on the shoulder. He said, "Well done!" I turned around, and it was Stephen Covey. I am so glad I didn't know he was right behind me, or I would have probably really blundered my introduction.

As the week went on, one of the seven habits had us writing our own Personal Mission Statement.

I would like to share with you, my family, and friends my Personal Mission Statement written in 1990.

9-18-90

Since this is a rough draft of my Personal Mission Statement, I will begin with my family.

I want to be the mother and grandmother that my children and grandchildren can be proud of.

I want to teach them the values of love, appreciation, respect for others, compassion, and loyalty, as well as to master them myself.

I want to be admired for this role and to be an example to them as my parents were to me. When you finish a job or task, look for something else to do! Pride of ownership—either small or large—is also important.

I want to be the friend and neighbor that shows respect and yet privacy to others. Don't infringe my beliefs and values on others even when I feel I am right. This, also, would apply to my family and all relationships.

I want to value the appreciation for all the cultural and finer things in my life. I have been truly blessed by a wonderful heritage and want that to continue through my children and grandchildren.

I hold close to me the freedoms I enjoy.

Also, I need to pay attention to the challenges in my life that have become obstacles. My health has to become more important. For if I can't function in my main roles I have outlined, I can be of no use or influence to anyone. If you don't have a healthy mind and body, you are unclear of exactly what your limits are.

I want to share with others the knowledge I have about leadership and management, life goals and stresses as I have grown from the obstacles and challenges I have overcome, either by choice or force.

I want to be a leader in my church and community by being an example of integrity and service.

I want to maintain a balance between what is really important in my life and choose which paths I will take and know the reasons I chose them and then be responsible for the actions I took and the decisions I made.

I will always strive to see the best in people and to express this love.

I want to speak and teach a group without fear.

May 27, 2023

Wow, thirty-three years later, I found this Personal Mission Statement in my files of personal papers. I have re-typed it here, changing only the words, my dad, to my parents. When I originally wrote this, my dad had passed away, and I was single, just getting over my second divorce.

As I read this, there isn't one thing I would change except to add in how important a good, solid marriage is to me. And, I have that now.

CHAPTER 15

Take what you do seriously,
but don't take yourself too seriously!

– Rita Davenport, GAMA presentation July 24, 2015

When I was younger, I took several years of organ lessons and played quite often. For the past several years, I hadn't practiced or even touched the organ—except to dust it.

I am the Music Chairman for our Ward which means I choose the songs and arrange for the chorister and organist each week. As I was preparing for the music several months ago, I realized the two women that usually play were both going to be out of town on this particular Sunday. So, I decided to dust off the organ, wiggle my fingers, step up, and volunteer to play on that day.

As I was preparing and practicing, I was a nervous wreck. Would I make mistakes, how would the organ be different than mine, how loud, how soft, and many other negative thoughts kept running through my head.

Several months prior to this, I had an experience with a man in my neighborhood I can only describe as a bully. He played the organ beautifully, and he played by ear. No one could play as well as him, and he let everyone know this. He was very critical of me and was outright rude to me on many occasions.

During my hours of practicing, I was full of doubts. Every time I thought of him and how he would be criticizing me, I would make a mistake.

The week before I was to play, a young lady was speaking in Church and read the story, *The Angel in Orange Boots*, by Emma Stanford. It was published in the *LDS Living Magazine*, December 2021.

It is a sweet story about a young girl who had been chosen to be an angel in her church Christmas performance of the Nativity. It was an outdoor production and was going to be very cold. She realized she needed some warm, heavy boots. Her mother took her shopping, and all they could find were some orange boots with red laces. She said they would survive an Antarctic expedition! She felt ridiculous in them, after all, what kind of angel wore orange boots?

What was to be a very peaceful experience for her was full of embarrassment even though she tried to hide her boots under her costume.

She said, "On the third night, I was waiting backstage with all the other angels, and I suddenly felt excited to share this final Nativity scene with the audience. I mean, *this was it*—the audience was going to *see angels* come in from all sides to kneel in front of the infant Savior. How incredible was that?

"I forgot all about my boots as the narrator recited Isaiah 9:6, which was my cue; 'For unto us a child is born, unto us a Son is given; and the government shall be upon his shoulder; and his name shall be called Wonderful, Counsellor, The Mighty God, The Everlasting Father, The Prince of Peace.

"As I walked out, everything else fell away. I felt like one of the heavenly angels—those powerful, glorified beings who were present at Christ's birth."

As the young lady finished, my friend leaned over to me and said, "You need to get a pair of orange boots!" I had shared with her my nervousness and concerns about playing the following week. I laughed and said I had been thinking the exact same thing.

I knew that in my rubber stamp stash, I had a stamp of rain boots. I came home and immediately made me a rubber-stamped print of the boots and colored them orange.

The morning I played, I had my own little version of my orange boots stuck on the music stand right by my music.

I realized I was playing for me, I was the only one I had to please, and I couldn't let his negativity come through and control my talent and performance.

I did great. Not sure how often I will play, but at least I know that I can! My colored orange boots still sit in a prominent spot on the organ in our home.

A few months after this experience, a family friend who had Parkinson's Disease sent out a message on his sixtieth birthday and challenged everyone to do sixty of something creative that would make a difference. I typed up the story of *The Angel in Orange Boots* and sent it out to sixty of my friends and a special thank you to he and his wife for their examples of love and service to so many.

CHAPTER 16

The greatest man I never knew.

I HAVE BEEN SO RICHLY BLESSED by my heritage—ancestors who came across the plains in covered wagon trains and walking, pulling handcarts. Many coming from Germany, England, Scotland, and Ireland spending days on ships and freighters to come to a land of freedom.

I have been asked several times about my childhood, growing up in Plain City, Utah.

I had a pretty normal childhood, a bratty little sister to my two older brothers. We lived in a home that had originally been a two-room log cabin. In 1864, there were two brothers and their families living in the home together. Later that year, the two brothers were called on Mormon Missions. The two wives worked hard and added a kitchen and two bedrooms to the home while the men were away.

I slept on a daybed in my parents' room until I was eight, then moved to my new bedroom—the dining room—and slept on a hideaway bed until we built our beautiful new home when I was thirteen. We didn't have a working bathroom until I was five.

In our new home, I had my own room with beautiful royal-blue plush carpet. I would take a little brush and brush it almost every day, making random designs in it.

Growing up in Plain City in the 1950s was the same as other small towns during those days.

I don't remember eating out at many restaurants. Maybe once in a while at Harmon's Kentucky Fried Chicken. I remember, however, almost every Wednesday night a smorgasbord at the Ogden Elks Lodge and being able to eat whatever we wanted. That was always a treat. Lunch with my mother at Z.C.M.I Tiffin Room was also a treat.

Shopping was also a fun memory with my mother. I remember Christmas, when I was eight years old, she bought me a new dress at L.R. Samuels on Washington Boulevard and made me promise to NEVER tell anyone how much it cost. It was $18.00. I loved that dress. It was purple with tiny white pearl buttons all the way down the front of it and a bow that tied in the back. This was the only special dress I remember ever having at a young age.

We would always eat as a family around our little yellow enamel kitchen table. We would eat what my mother had prepared, and I never remember complaining or refusing to eat anything.

We would play games outside with our friends for hours and ride our bikes, but always knew when it got dark, we'd better get home.

In 1959, many special memories began. My dad and

several other men in Plain City bought 1959 Glass Craft, fifteen-foot boats. They were all the same model boat, but each was a different color. Ours was red, other families had turquoise, peach/pink, and yellow. Every Sunday, we would load up our picnics of bologna sandwiches, mother's homemade potato and macaroni salads, and head to Pineview Dam. We had so much fun but had to be home by 5 o'clock for my dad to watch *Bonanza* or *Maverick*.

I recently heard a story on the news about a lady that was giving away free helmets at a local sledding hill. I understand that there are indeed safety issues with sledding but it made me remember another fun memory and we certainly didn't have helmets.

It was Christmas Eve, probably 1965. My brother, Jerry brought home the old hood of an old car. He had it upside down pulling it behind his car. My mother piled old blankets on it and we were off. Sledding through the snow packed streets of Plain City on that crisp night on an upside down hood of an old car. Nope, no helmets that night, and yet we all survived.

Shortly after we returned home we heard beautiful sleigh bells and here came our dear friend and neighbor, Dean Baker with his team of horses pulling a sleigh. He was going across everyone's snow covered yards so they could see that Santa had indeed come that night.

My parents were honest, hardworking, fun-loving people. My two brothers, Jerry and Ronald, have been powerful influences and examples of hard work, generosity, and fun in my life. I feel like I had a perfect childhood.

After my dad got out of the service in 1945, he drove a truck with Eugene England. These two men, along with their sons, started what are now two of the largest trucking companies in the U.S., Swift Transportation and C.R. England Trucking. There is a movie on YouTube called *Diesel In The Water* about the beginning of these trucking empires being started in Plain City, Utah.

After my dad passed away, we realized while he was in the service, he was in the O.S.S. which is the Office of Strategic Services, the beginning of the CIA. We did not know what he did in the service, except he always told us he was a chauffeur. My Uncle Lewis told us a story he had always remembered as a young boy that my dad had shared.

He was driving a semitruck from Washington, DC, to San Francisco. The trip was to take several days. He had no paperwork on the heavily locked load and did not know what he was transporting. All he knew was when he stopped every night at an assigned location, he had heavily armed guards surrounding the truck and trailer. When he finally got to San Francisco and was ready to unload, he asked, "What in the hell am I hauling?" As they opened the back doors of the trailer, he saw he was transporting a forty-foot trailer full of the finest whiskey made. It was a delivery to prepare for what was to be the first United Nations meeting in April 1945.

My dad passed away too early in his life. He was only sixty-five and died from complications from prostate and back cancer. Two days before he passed away, my mother received a call from the hospital nurse telling her my dad was calling for her. We rushed to the hospital to find him very lucid. He told us he was going to die that day because, he said, "I have seen something more beautiful, and it made me realize I don't need to lay here and suffer." Wow, for my dad to say this, we were all shocked. He slipped into a coma later that day and passed away the next. My mother truly believed he did see something more beautiful, or he never would have said it. My dad was a firm man who many would explain as an observer. He was a man of very few words, but when he spoke, you listened.

Dad loved to play cards. Gin Rummy was his game. My mom and dad were members of both the Ogden Elks Lodge and the Ogden Golf and Country Club. One day, a man came into the office where I worked to see my boss. When my boss introduced me as Carl Moyes's daughter, the man said, laughing, "Hell, we all decided it would be cheaper to buy your dad an airplane ticket back to Phoenix than to play a game of cards with him." Dad was good. When he passed away, we found several uncashed checks in his wallet from men who had played cards with him and lost.

A few nights before he went to the hospital for the last time, I was playing cards with him, and I actually won a game. I'm not sure if he was just too sick to realize it, but it was an honest win. One thing I learned from him about playing cards was to never speculate. I try to remember that even today when I am playing cards with Roger!

Reba McEntire's song, "The Greatest Man I Never Knew" truly reminds me of my dad.

> The greatest man I never knew
> Lived just down the hall
> And every day we said, "Hello"
> But never touched at all
> He was in his paper
> I was in my room
> How was I to know he thought I hung the moon?
>
> The greatest man I never knew
> Came home late every night
> He never had too much to say
> Too much was on his mind
> I never really knew him
> Oh, and now it seems so sad
> Everything he gave us, took all he had
>
> Then the days turned into years
> And the memories to black and white
> He grew cold like an old winter wind
> Blowing across my life
>
> The greatest words I never heard
> I guess I'll never hear
> The man I thought could never die
> Has been dead almost a year
>
> Oh, he was good at business
> But there was business left to do
> He never said he loved me
> Guess he thought I knew

Oh, I had a beautiful mother. She continued to live a very active life, traveling and visiting family and friends after Dad passed away. She quietly passed away at eighty-two after a brief illness. She was the most kind, beautiful woman who loved everyone. Oh, of course, there were a few who crossed her, but she would move on—a few cuss words and a few hand gestures would escape her, and we would all laugh.

They are both so missed.

She was famous for many recipes, but two of them that are always requested are her Grandma Betty Sugar Cookies and her Grandma Betty Famous Lemon Jello Salad.

When she was in Phoenix, she would make several batches of the cookies, bag them up, and take them to my niece's and nephew's places of work and actually have the individuals' names on the ones that she wanted to have some. It was always a joke because she would bring them in, and they would eat all the cookies before her favorite people would have any. That was why she started putting names on the baggies.

We even shared the recipe on her funeral program. A few weeks after the funeral, a lady called me and said she was trying to make the cookies and there was no liquid. She asked me if she was doing something wrong. I looked at the program and realized we had forgotten to add "3 eggs" to the recipe. By this time, it had been printed in the local Phoenix newspaper, so they had to re-print her recipe, stating there had been a secret missing ingredient.

Grandma Betty Sugar Cookies

1 Cup Butter Flavored Shortening (Crisco) (or Butter)

1 1/2 Cup Sugar

1 Tablespoon Vanilla

3 1/2 Cups Flour

3 Eggs

1 Teaspoon Cream of Tarter

1 Teaspoon Baking Soda

1/2 Teaspoon Salt

- Mix all of the ingredients together and refrigerate the dough for one hour or even overnight.
- Roll into 1-inch balls and place two inches apart on a cookie sheet.
- Bake at 375 degrees for 8–10 minutes.

FROSTING:

1 8 ounce package Cream Cheese

1/4 Cup Melted Butter

1 Pound package of Powder Sugar

1/2 Teaspoon Vanilla (or Almond Flavoring)

Drips of food coloring for color

Grandma Betty Famous Lemon Jello Salad

1 Large Package of Lemon Jello

2 Cups Boiling Water

2 Cups 7-Up or Sprite

- Prepare the Jello as stated on the box only using the 7-Up instead of the cold water.
- Let partially set.
- Drain and SAVE the juice from a 20 oz. can of crushed pineapple and stir the pineapple into the partially set Jello. After it is set, add 1 1/2 cup miniature marshmallows and three sliced bananas to the top.

TOPPING: Mix 1 Cup Pineapple juice, 1 beaten egg, 2 T. Flour, 1 T. Butter and 1/2 Cup sugar.

- Bring these ingredients to a boil. Let sit for 5 minutes and refrigerate. About an hour before serving, mix with 1 cup of prepared whipped cream and spread on top of the salad.

CHAPTER 17

I believe there are angels among us.

RECENTLY, Roger and I were asked to speak in church.

When the Bishop asked us to talk, he suggested we talk about how Christ has affected our lives, how he has strengthened us through our challenges, and given us greater purpose. "Just let the spirit be your guide," he said.

I started looking at General Conference talks for inspiration. I was reading through different ones in the *Ensign*, a church magazine, and found Elder Jeffery R. Holland's talk on the ministering of angels and decided that was where I would focus my thoughts.

I have always had a curiosity and fascination with angels; how they minister to us and how we can also be angels to minister to others.

Parts of my talk follow with some quotes from Elder Holland:

> After my second marriage, and years went by, I made some selfish choices in my life that eventu-

ally caused me to be excommunicated from the Church of Jesus Christ of Latter-day Saints. It was through special friends, and I know, loving angels, that my son at age sixteen decided he wanted to become active in the church. He had friends that he saw a light in them, and he wanted that in his life. Through a lot of prayer, fasting, repentance, and examples of many friends, I was able to get baptized again, and my son was able to baptize me. I had several of the Layton High Football team sing at my baptism, "Because I Have Been Given Much I Too Must Give." This is a song that even today makes me cry when I hear it. I also asked the Bishop I had when I was excommunicated, DeLynn Yeates, to speak at my baptism.

Blessings? Angels? I cannot deny that!

I have had several brushes with death. As I said earlier, my mother used to call me her daughter with nine lives and would tell me to be careful, especially when I was traveling. She said, "God really must have something special in mind for you." Perhaps, that something special is I am able to stand here today and share with you.

Several of these experiences, I know, were witnessed by angels who were right there by my side.

Angels can guide.

I'm sure angels can even laugh.

Usually, such beings are not seen. Sometimes, they are. But, seen or unseen, they are always near. Sometimes, their assignments are grand and have significance for the entire world, but other times, their messages are more private. Occasionally, their purpose is to warn, but most often, it is to comfort, to provide some form of merciful attention and guidance in difficult times.

I mentioned earlier about my friend asking me if perhaps the nurse at the side of the road, dressed in white, could have been my guardian angel. As time went on, I realized and truly believe that yes, she was indeed my guardian angel, and I believe I know who she is.

In August of 1964, I was fourteen. I had done some temple baptism work in the Logan LDS Temple. One of the names I was baptized for was Mary Barefoot. I have always remembered that name and remember writing it in a little journal that afternoon when I got home. No one I have ever talked to about this can ever remember any names they had been baptized for, especially that long ago. I am convinced beyond any shadow of a doubt the lady I thought was a nurse on the edge of the water that night in Florida was Mary Barefoot. I tried researching her on Ancestry and Family Search to see if there was a photo of her. With the help of a friend, I was able to find her information, but she was born in the early 1600s, so there were no photos.

When I found her actual name, it was Mary Barfoote, a name I probably would have never remembered, but as the Temple worker read her name, Mary Barefoot, I knew I could never forget that name.

From that night until today, my life has been so richly blessed by angels on both sides of the veil that came into my life at just the right time.

Another sweet story about angels that touched me deeply took place in November 2018.

On a beautiful fall day in October 2018, my cousin's wife was traveling between Richfield and her home in Teasdale, Utah. She hit a deer and was killed in the accident, leaving her sweet husband and three small children. A few weeks later, her son, CJ, was to be baptized, so Roger and I went over for his baptism. The baptism and confirmation were held at the Historic Loa Tabernacle, in

Loa, Utah. As the Primary room started to fill, more people continued to come. We then moved to the Relief Society room, and it filled to overflow also. They were going to move into the chapel, and some of those who were standing said they were fine and to move on with the baptism.

As we moved into the baptismal room and witnessed the baptism, I was so filled with emotion I could hardly contain my tears. After the baptism, we moved back into the Relief Society room for the confirmation. The spirit was so strong. As his daddy started the confirmation, he placed his hands on CJ's head and said, "Cody James Clark, by the power of the Melchizedek Priesthood, I..." and he stopped.

For what seemed like several minutes, he was struggling to continue. The room was silent, and as I sat there with my head bowed, eyes closed, and arms folded, I thought to myself, "Don't open your eyes because this entire room is filled to the ceiling with angels." He then got his composure back and continued with the most beautiful confirmation blessing I had ever witnessed.

Several weeks later, I was at a friend's home and saw a painting on her wall, and it stopped me right there. That is what I witnessed in the room that night. It was a painting of angels comforting a lady. It is titled, *She Will Find What Is Lost* by Brian Kershisnik.

Our present days are filled with so much heartache, distresses, family concerns over finances, our homes, our health, our family safety. These translate into concerns not only for our families but the ultimate safety and well-being of our children. More serious than these, and sometimes related to them, are matters of ethical, moral, and spiritual decay seen in populations large and small, at home and abroad. "But," Elder Holland said, "I testify that angels are still sent to help us."

How has Christ affected my life? How has he strengthened me through my challenges and given me greater purpose? By placing angels on both sides of the veil to protect and help guide me. By helping me know when to listen and be ever mindful to watch for opportunities to be an angel to someone in need. To always watch for the angels around me and learn to love and appreciate the rich blessings in my life as I strive to continue to live the Gospel of Jesus Christ.

What are the lessons I have learned throughout my life? I have learned tolerance. I have learned forgiveness, humility, integrity, how to be more generous, how to grieve, how to both give and receive service, how to love others, and also to learn to love myself.

ACKNOWLEDGEMENTS

WITHOUT THE SUPPORT from my family and friends, this book would not exist. You have supported me from day one. For those not mentioned here, you know who you are!

I want to thank my awesome husband Roger. From the beginning, you have been so supportive of this endeavor. You helped me by reading my original drafts and making many helpful suggestions. I remember well the night in Mexico I had to make my final decision on my cover design. You sat by my side for what seemed like hours, helping me pick the best design.

Thank you again for replying to my original Facebook message ten years ago.

I want to thank my children, Michelle, Chad, and their families for allowing me to share my story, and with it being my story, it also makes it theirs. We survived in spite of everything!

I am so grateful for the Author Ready program and the friends I have made at the writer's retreats at the Timepiece Ranch. Your friendships and encouragement also made this book more important to complete.

Thanks also to Toni Asay, Professor at Weber State College. She started me out on my editing process, and I am so grateful to her for her proofreading work, suggestions, and most of all, her friendship.

I also want to thank Kim Autrey for her copy editing and the hours spent helping me to complete my work. I think she took out at least 100 "that's."

Many thanks to Rita Davenport for her help in getting me the permission from Reba McEntire to print the words to the song, "The Greatest Man I Never Knew." This song has always reminded me of my dad and the special man he was.

I also want to thank Francine Platt at Eden Graphics, for her work on the interior design. She, too, took many phone calls from me helping me along my journey to completion.

From Jakarta, Indonesia, I want to thank Ruth with ElQue Designs / 99Designs for her winning book cover design. I had over 600 submissions, and hers was my favorite from the beginning.

A very special thank you to Reba McEntire for allowing me to use the words to her heartwarming song about fathers, "The Greatest Man I Never Knew."

And lastly, to Richard Paul Evans for his mentorship, friendship, and love for what he does. He has helped so many complete their dreams of writing, and I am one more to add to that list. From my first day at the Writer's Retreat to every phone call, you have made me feel like my story is one to share and encouraged me to get there. Thank You!

ENDNOTES

Prologue

1. Google search, s.v. "Resilience."

Chapter 5

1. Rachel Marie Martin, "Sometimes you have to let go of the picture of what you thought life would be like and learn to find joy in the story you're actually living", Facebook, November 3, 2023, https://m.facebook.com/photo.php?fbid=856553549810942&set=a.494525546013746&type=3#_=_

Chapter 6

1. "Because I Have Been Given Much, I Too Must Give" (No. 219) in Hymns (Salt Lake City, UT, The Church of Jesus Christ of Latter-day Saints, 1992).

   Text: Grace Noll Cowell 1877-1969

   Music: Phillip Landgave

   LDS Hymn Book

Chapter 8

1. Doe Zantamata, "Good friends help you to find important things when you have lost them…Your smile, your hope and your courage," Facebook, January 27, 2012, https://www.facebook.com/Happinessinyourlife/photos/a.225250587555673/238146606266071/?type=3&paipv=0&eav=Afb3PtjTYqUV8HY-l0ycxH82Wxekvt47fMun1hgbIoMd9XgFLOFa-b_WwhILm-6FK9Obk&_rdr.

Chapter 10

1. Nanea Hoffman, "If today gets difficult, remember the smell of coffee, the way sunlight bounces off a window, the sound of your favorite person's laugh," Instagram photo, May 3, 2022, https://www.instagram.com/p/CdGgEAEDVo-/.